Tomato

80 Recipes Celebrating
the Extraordinary Tomato

CLAIRE THOMSON

photography by Sam Folan

Hardie Grant

QUADRILLE

FOR GRACE, IVY AND DOROTHY

'You to me are everything'

Contents

'Every week most of us will be making use of tomatoes in one form or other several times.'
Jane Grigson

As I write the introduction to this cookbook, it is the tail end of summer. Sitting on my kitchen table is a bowl brimming bright and full of tomatoes – my writing stimulus, all shapes and sizes. The stems and leaves are pungent and grassy; the fruit sweet, almost spicy. Outside, the daylight has a plush, golden glow to it – gone is the searing white light of summer and, in its place, a new, early autumn light.

I've spent these last summer months eating an awful lot of tomatoes – thankfully a favourite ingredient of mine, bringing me, as they do, a particular joy. A summer fruit, their culinary use straddles the seasons, proving them a vital, year-round ingredient. In the name of research, I've consumed kilos and kilos this summer, unendingly and voraciously, in so many different dishes. But now, today, with the season changing, so too is my tomato use.

I thrive on these cycles of cookery. Now is the time I find myself switching out my sharp knife that has sliced and chopped tomatoes daily over the summer months, for a can opener. Or, I catch myself flexing to open a jar or lid to make use of canned or processed tomato products. I begin to seek richer, warmer flavours in the food I cook. Any especially industrious cooks among us might get busy processing a ripe glut, or finding use for a green one – the taut, unruly stragglers that failed ever to ripen.

The act of preserving fresh goods to use later in the year is a romantic one. The practice stems from what was once a necessity to stock up the store cupboard for winter. And, while the making of sauces, jams and chutneys continues to be habitual for many, others might view it as an indulgence for people interested in cookery, and perhaps gardening, and with time to spare. Whatever the catalyst for it, the moment of opening a jar or bottle of tomato-something, thoughtfully produced when the ingredient was in its prime in readiness for a future when it's scarce, is transportive – it's like bottled time.

This was always going to be a book of two halves – fresh tomatoes and processed tomatoes – giving plenty of opportunity for both to really shine. I'm duty bound to encourage you to steer clear of freighted, out-of-season fruit – all you need to do is to switch from fresh to preserved and back again, as the seasons dictate.

Introduction

Which Tomatoes? Why Tomatoes?

From a flavour perspective, tomatoes require sunshine and warmth and time on the vine to really develop deeply. Ideally, the best tomatoes are grown outside, in blazing heat, with plenty of water given during the growing period, less when the plant has fruited. With these perfect growing conditions, the plants will thrive, the fruit intensifying in flavour and improving in texture, until ready to harvest. Here in the UK, and increasingly elsewhere, our inclement summer weather means that some growers are grateful for greenhouses and the protection these bring against the elements.

Tomatoes are one of a handful of ingredients that envelop four of the five flavour profiles – sweet, sour, bitter and umami. The fifth is salt, which we all know tomatoes carry beautifully. Sprinkle a slice of perfectly ripe tomato with some good salt and this is a most complete mouthful, perfect in every way.

Crucially, cooked in dishes, tomatoes provide body, enriching a sauce as it bubbles, the tomatoes breaking down and thickening to give viscosity – a result that is luscious in form. If you blend a tomato sauce that has been cooked in oil or butter, for example, you will end up with something deeply creamy and velvety.

Processed tomatoes, by which I mean canned, bottled or puréed, are not inferior to fresh, and outside of your domestic growing season, I would encourage you to use the best-quality processed tomatoes you can – they will taste better. Look for plum tomatoes – San Marzano, in particular. I also like to use canned cherry tomatoes. The contents of every can – plum or cherry – are made up of two separate ingredients: the tomatoes themselves (usually four or five plum tomatoes, if that's what you're using) and the juice. You can use the entire contents of a can, or, if you want to use canned tomatoes like you would fresh (perhaps in a cooked dish), you can pop them in to cook without the juice – but do save the juice for a later date. Processed tomatoes have already been cooked just a little to preserve them, which means they taste more intense than their fresh equivalents. As for tomato purée, think of this as concentrated tomato: the good stuff should taste great, just as it is, squeezed straight from the tube… like tomatoes left to dry in the sun for maximum flavour.

A Very Brief History of the Tomato

The tomato is the edible fruit of the *Solanum lycopersicum* plant, a member of a diverse group of flowering plants, known collectively as Solanaceae, which includes potatoes and aubergines. Solanaceae are associated with the highly poisonous belladonna or deadly nightshade family. An inauspicious start for the tomato, you might think.

Native to western South America, tomatoes' colossal use in much of the world's diet today tells us a lot about their historical and cultural significance as a food and in cookery. Once a wild plant, with green-yellow and diminutive fruit, thought to have grown only in and around the western region of South America (Peru, Ecuador and Bolivia, specifically), the tomato appears to have been first cultivated during the Aztec Empire (1345–1521) in central Mexico. Through their sophisticated approach to agriculture, the Aztecs migrated their crops, accelerating the cultivation of the fruit and, ultimately, rendering tomatoes crucial to Mexican, and indeed all South American, cuisine.

In 1521, Hernán Cortés, a Spanish conquistador, led an invasion that ultimately caused the fall of the Aztec Empire. As a result, the tomato plant (along with other seedlings for prize crops such as chillies, vanillas, beans and corn) found itself gathered and stored for travel across the Atlantic, aboard ships bound for Europe. Among the plants and seedlings were unprecedented levels of gold and silver – unsurprisingly, as a result of this ill-gotten bounty, Spain grew exceptionally rich.

It is fascinating, then, given the tomato plant's arrival on Europe's shores as the booty of mercenaries, and its association with the deadly nightshade family, to contemplate just how popular the fruit became and in just how much of the world. From Spain to the rest of Europe, and from there to the Middle East, Africa, Asia (China is now the biggest tomato-producing country in all the world) and Australia/Oceania, the tomato is prevalent in myriad regional cuisines – almost as if everyone, the world over, wants to claim it as their own. Food culture seems to have cast a positively critical eye on tomatoes, and said, yes, we're having those.

I find the trajectory and timeline of tomatoes – of when and where they were used as an ingredient in the world – remarkable. Throughout history and across cultures, humans have proved themselves to have an unending thirst for new ingredients, both for the ingredients' health benefits (tomatoes are packed with disease-fighting antioxidants) and as a food source. The provenance of the tomato plant highlights, for me, the fact that many ingredients (and, by extension, recipes) have been appropriated. I want to note here that recipes that come from a country not my own are inviolable – thanks only to the people who have handed them onwards, through writing or action. Documenting the lineage and crediting the heritage of recipes is critical. In bringing this book together, I want to acknowledge rather than sidestep the notion of appropriation in cookery – and to do so with humility for the fact that I am writing a book on tomatoes and yet have never set foot on South American soil. Nonetheless, in this book I hope my love for tomatoes rings proud and true.

Tomatoes, Give Me All Tomatoes

This book covers the whole gamut of tomato cookery, from too-hot-to-cook days, when you might find yourself slicing fresh tomatoes and assembling them together with simpatico ingredients (never really cooking, more a case of intuition and action) to more protracted tasks that result in a pan simmering on the stove top. Seasonal change and your preferred cooking techniques will decide what ingredients you pair with them.

At the last count there were 10,000 tomato varieties identified in the world. For the purposes of the recipes in this book, I've used the simple classification of 'tomatoes', sometimes listing cherry tomatoes, if appropriate. For a medium sized, red, ripe tomato I've estimated this to weigh in at 100g, or thereabouts. I've done this to keep things simple for the cook; I want people to feel empowered and enthusiastic, to get stuck into these recipes, with whatever tomatoes they have to hand. Tomatoes are a forgiving ingredient, so I feel it best to not be too bossy on varietal use. I've used only whole plum canned tomatoes (for chopped, I simply open the can and scissor the lot inside it), and some canned cherry tomatoes for when I want tomatoes to appear in a complete but smaller format. And, finally, there are recipes with passata and some with purée.

Deep in the vortex of compiling and cooking these 80 tomato recipes, I found myself entranced by just how wonderful an ingredient a tomato is. Tomatoes really have proved themselves to be one of my top three ingredients (the other two, since you ask, are olive oil and lemons). I could not be without them. In the last six months, in the name of research I have consumed a gargantuan 75 kilos of fresh tomatoes all from the Isle of Wight (tomato growers I have been collaborating with), plus the tomatoes I have bought from my local greengrocer, plus more from my stepfather's greenhouse, plus almost 100 cans of tomatoes and a case (that is, 25 tubes!) of tomato purée. The phrase 'labour of love' was never more true than in the writing of this book. The work that has gone into it has seen extreme determination – from my children too – in the face of so many tomatoes. Yet, I know we've barely skated across the tip of the iceberg when it comes to tomato production and consumption.

I will stand by the fact that my favourite kitchen task of all time is to make a nick on the skin of a perfectly ripe, but still firm, fresh tomato, then plunge it into rolling, boiling water for 10 seconds. Then, to immediately transfer the tomato to a bowl of iced water, leaving it for 10 seconds, only for the skin to slip easily away like thickly waxed paper. What emerges is a flesh that is smooth, pink-tinged and almost iridescent. As prep jobs go, this one is almost meditative. I could stand there for hours, like Rapunzel spinning straw into gold, but instead me (or you) spinning tomatoes into something sublime.

With 180 million tonnes of tomatoes grown globally, it's clear that the appetite for this extraordinary fruit that masquerades determinedly as a vegetable, flaunting its versatility, is undiminishable. It has been my complete pleasure to write this book, without doubt my love letter to tomatoes.

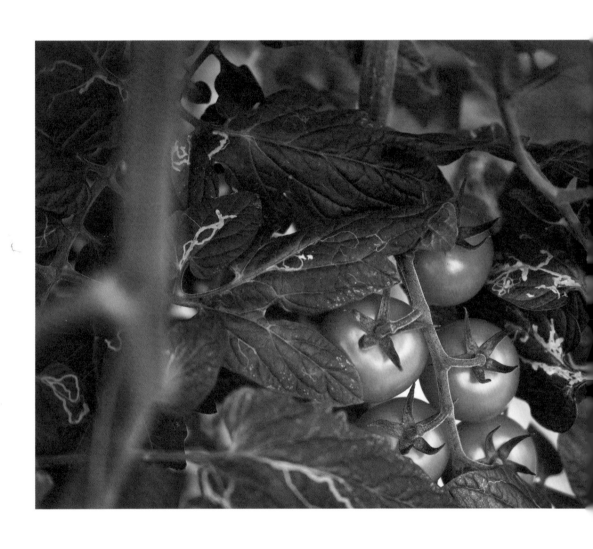

This is the chapter to tackle when fresh tomatoes are in season... homegrown, cultivated patiently in pots in the garden or on sills in the window, or cheaply bought from the greengrocer – and lots of them. You will likely want a good load of fresh tomatoes, taut and teeming with promise, for most of these recipes. Some are an invitation to bottle for use later on in the year, others are there for you to consume with enthusiasm when tomatoes are plentiful. The tomato is king of the condiments, offering ripe, sweet, fleshy fruit that pairs brilliantly with various other ingredients to make some of our most favourite spices, chillies, sour additions, oils and sugars. These are flavours that encourage us to shake or spoon great dollops on to our plates, ramping up flavour in the food we all want to eat.

Condiments

Tomato Chutney

800g (1lb 12oz) tomatoes, stalks
    removed and roughly chopped
2 large shallots or 1 onion, finely
    chopped
2cm (¾in) piece of fresh ginger, finely
    grated (shredded)
2 garlic cloves, finely chopped
450g (1lb) caster (superfine) sugar
200ml (7fl oz) white wine vinegar

1 teaspoon salt, plus more to season
1 teaspoon freshly ground black pepper,
    plus more to season
pinch of chilli flakes, or more to taste
½ teaspoon ground cinnamon
1 teaspoon ground cumin
1 clove
2 bay leaves

Chutney originated in India, using an age-old process devised to store fresh ingredients for enjoying at a later date, preserving with sugar, vinegar and spices, among other ingredients. Chutney-making, as it is today and now throughout much of the world, is a much-loved and common kitchen task. Served as condiment to a wide variety of savoury dishes, chutney likes to be stored for a good month before use, giving it time for the flavours to meld and helping to round off sharp corners. You need scrupulously clean jars for storing the chutney, so don't skip the first step!

1. Sterilize your jars. Wash them in very hot soapy water or on the hot cycle of a dishwasher. Preheat the oven to 160°C/140°C fan/315°F/Gas 2–3. Rinse the jars and place them upside down on a baking sheet and heat them in the oven for 10 minutes. Boil the kettle and pour boiling water over the lids to sterilize. Keep to one side with a clean, dry tea towel over the lot.

2. Put all the chutney ingredients into a large saucepan.

3. Bring the mixture to a boil over a medium–high heat and simmer vigorously for 10 minutes, seasoning with salt and pepper, to taste.

4. Reduce the heat to a low simmer and cook gently, stirring often, for about 1–1½ hours, until the chutney is thick and glossy. Remove the clove if it's easy to locate, not to worry if you can't track it down. Remove the bay leaves.

5. Remove the pan from the heat and carefully decant the chutney into the sterilized jars. Seal tightly with the sterilized lids and store in a cool, dry place. Sealed and stored correctly, the chutney should last indefinitely but is best consumed within a year. Once opened, store in the fridge and consume within a month or two.

Hot Sauce

6-10 Scotch bonnet or habanero chillies, stems removed, roughly chopped

300g (10½oz) plum or cherry tomatoes, roughly chopped

250g (9oz) pineapple, skin removed, cored and roughly diced

8 garlic cloves, roughly chopped

1 small onion, roughly chopped

100ml (3½fl oz) white wine vinegar or cider vinegar

2 teaspoons salt

Hot sauce is terrible stuff – truly. So very addictive. I have been known to veto its use from time to time, at least to give some other condiments table space. I find there are not many dishes that aren't improved by a splash, a slosh, and soon enough bottles and bottles of the stuff begin to accumulate in the cupboard or fridge. You've been warned... Luckily though, it is quite easy to make. Hot sauces are made in many countries throughout the world, hot from the variety of chillies used, of course, and often with added fruit for bulk and a beguiling fruitiness. Tomatoes are the fruit in this one, for their juicy, fruity weight, but I'm also adding a ripe pineapple for extra tang and sweetness. Scotch bonnet chillies, a flat-bottomed and fairly diminutive-looking chilli, ubiquitous in West African and Caribbean cooking, and also called 'Jamaican hots', are related to the habanero. They are extremely hot, but also have a good fruitiness.

This sauce will keep for up to two weeks in the fridge. It will not last indefinitely because it has relatively low sugar and vinegar levels. That said, it is still wise to sterilize the jars or bottles. Halve the recipe, if you like, or make some to give away to friends.

1. Sterilize the jars. Wash them in very hot soapy water or on the hot cycle of a dishwasher. Preheat the oven to 160°C/140°C fan/315°F/Gas 2-3. Rinse the jars and place them upside down on a baking sheet and heat them in the oven for 10 minutes. Boil the kettle and pour boiling water over the lids to sterilize. Keep to one side with a clean, dry tea towel over the lot.

2. Combine all the ingredients for the hot sauce together with 150ml (5fl oz) of water in a non-reactive saucepan. Place the pan over a high heat and bring to a rapid boil, then reduce the heat and cook at a low simmer, uncovered, for 30 minutes. Remove from the heat.

3. Using a good blender, process the sauce until completely smooth. For a runnier sauce, you can add a splash of freshly boiled water. I don't bother – my hot sauce is the same consistency as regular ketchup.

4. Once the sauce is smooth, carefully decant it into the sterilized jars. Cool, then store in the fridge for up to two weeks.

CONDIMENTS

Ketchup *(pictured overleaf)*

4kg (8lb 12oz) tomatoes, roughly
  chopped
2 onions, roughly chopped
4 garlic cloves, roughly chopped
250ml (9fl oz) cider vinegar
150ml (5fl oz) malt vinegar
200g (7oz) light muscovado sugar
1 tablespoon salt
1 teaspoon English mustard

1 heaped teaspoon ground cloves
1 teaspoon ground allspice
½ teaspoon ground ginger
1 x 7cm (2¾in) cinnamon stick
1 heaped teaspoon celery salt
1 teaspoon ground white or black pepper

Iconic is the ketchup bottle, a bright, conspicuous red, squeezing thick stripes or noisy squirts, sweet and salty. Most children, and plenty of adults too, have an involuntary reflex with ketchup, a need to return to the bottle a second, a third, a who-am-I-to-judge time, adding more (and yet more) ketchup still to whatever ingredient is sidekick. As ketchup is easy to come by in the shops, making it is not an essential activity. Rather, it is a task to master when you have too many tomatoes you know what to – hang on – know perfectly well what to do with. Making your own ketchup isn't intended as some puffed-up activity, it is economical and sensible, using ingredients that are ripe and ready in profusion, and giving them a lifeline beyond just the next few days. Homemade ketchup... well, it's got to taste like the shop-bought stuff really, hasn't it?

1. Sterilize your jars. Wash them in very hot soapy water or on the hot cycle of a dishwasher. Preheat the oven to 160°C/140°C fan/315°F/Gas 2–3. Rinse the jars and place them upside down on a baking sheet and heat them in the oven for 10 minutes. Boil the kettle and pour boiling water over the lids to sterilize. Keep to one side with a clean, dry tea towel over the lot.

2. Put the tomatoes, onions and garlic in a large, heavy-based saucepan. Add the remaining ingredients and place the pan over a moderate–high heat. Bring the contents of the pan to a boil, making sure you stir all the while to help dissolve the sugar.

3. Reduce the heat to the merest blip and cook for a further 2½–3½ hours. Be vigilant – you don't want the bottom to stick and the ingredients to catch; stir vigorously from time to time.

4. When it's ready, the mixture should be well cooked and integrated and very soupy in appearance. Take the pan off the heat and remove the cinnamon stick.

5. Carefully blitz the mixture in a blender until smooth. Pass it through a fine-mesh sieve and really squeeze and push it through using the back of a ladle into a large, clean saucepan. Discard the skin and pip debris in the sieve when you are sure you have thoroughly squeezed out as much of the mixture as you can.

6. Bring the sieved sauce to a vigorous simmer over a moderate-high heat and season well with extra salt and pepper, as you like. Be careful – the mixture will spit and bubble volcanically from time to time. Simmer for about 4–5 minutes, stirring carefully and continuously.

7. Remove from the heat and carefully decant into the sterilized jars.

8. Sealed and stored correctly, the ketchup should last indefinitely but is best consumed within a year. Once opened, store in the fridge and consume within a month or two.

Tomato and Chilli Jam

MAKES 3
JARS (ABOUT
450G/1LB EACH)

1.5kg (3lb 5oz) tomatoes
1.5kg (3lb 5oz) granulated sugar
1 large bramley apple, peeled, cored
  and diced small

1 red chilli (mild or hot, as you like),
  halved (optional)
2 cardamom pods
juice of 1 large lemon

This recipe showcases the tomato as a fruit intended for making great jam. You'll need to skin the tomatoes (easy enough, you have my word), but what you then end up with is a knock-out beautiful jar of translucent, ruby-red jelly with the seeds suspended throughout, along with dots of fresh chilli and cardamom. Use it as a condiment for when you want a sweet, hot hit on anything grilled (burgers or halloumi would be ideal); with more fiery dishes, where you want the sweetness of the tomato jam to melt and lift a dish, in a stir-fry, for example; or for when you want to add a dash of sweetness to a braise or stew, rounding flavour in the finished sauce. Original recipe published by The Tomato Stall (@iowtomatoes) and reprinted here with their kind permission.

1. Sterilize your jars. Wash them in very hot soapy water or on the hot cycle of a dishwasher. Preheat the oven to 160°C/140°C fan/315°F/Gas 2–3. Rinse the jars and place them upside down on a baking sheet and heat them in the oven for 10 minutes. Boil the kettle and pour boiling water over the lids to sterilize. Keep to one side with a clean, dry tea towel over the lot.

2. Have a big pan of water boiling. Working in batches, slash the skin of each tomato with a sharp knife and plunge a few into the boiling water for 10 seconds. Remove with a slotted spoon and put to one side. Keep going until you've blanched them all. Leave to cool slightly (no need to plunge them into cold water at this stage, as I've described elsewhere in this book). The skins should now slip off easily – peel all the tomatoes and discard the skin.

3. Roughly chop all the skinned tomatoes and place them in a deep pan suitable for making jam. Add the sugar and apple and mix well. Let the mixture sit for 30 minutes. Add the chilli, if using, and the cardamom pods and lemon juice.

4. Put the pan on the heat and bring the mixture to a rapid boil. Be careful – it will be very, very hot. Boil until the mixture reaches 105°C/220°F on a digital thermometer. Alternatively, put a plate in the freezer when you begin the jam-making process and, when the bubbles on the jam appear fatter and more viscous (anytime from about 20 minutes of boiling), test a spoonful of jam on the cold plate – if it is ready, it should thicken instantly and have a slight skin to the top if you push it with your finger. A digital thermometer is best, though. At this point boil the jam hard for 2 minutes for a perfect set.

5. Remove the pan from the heat and carefully pour the jam into the sterilized jars, removing the chillies and cardamom pods, if you like (or keep them in – up to you). Seal tightly with the sterilized lids. Sealed and stored correctly, the jam should last indefinitely. Once opened, store in the fridge and consume within a month or two.

Burnt Tomato Salsa

600g (1lb 5oz) tomatoes
6 garlic cloves, skin on
1 red onion, quartered and peeled
  (stalk left intact)
½ small bunch of coriander (cilantro),
  roughly chopped

1–2 limes (depending on juiciness)
1 dried arbol or pequin chilli, or another
  medium-hot dried chilli (or fresh red
  or green chilli, if you prefer)
salt and freshly ground black pepper

*Burning the tomatoes, onions, chilli and whole garlic cloves with their skin on in a dry
pan or on a grill or barbecue does two things in the making of this salsa. First, the heat
distorts the skin and flesh, rendering all four ingredients soft enough to roughly peel,
then chop as one mass, all seasoned with lime and a good amount of salt. Second,
by heating the ingredients and blistering the skin, ideally, you're looking to burn and
blacken parts of the flesh of each, lending deeply smoky notes to the flesh within.
Pair with Mexican food, including tacos, quesadillas and burritos, or enjoy as part
of a larger meal such as barbacoa or any long, slow-cooked South American dishes.*

1. Grill the whole tomatoes, garlic and quartered onions over a high heat in a dry pan
for about 10 minutes, turning every now and then, until blistered, well charred and
blackened in places. Remove from the heat and leave to cool.

2. Remove the skins from the tomatoes and garlic.

3. Finely chop the charred vegetables together and season with salt and pepper, then
add the coriander (cilantro), along with plenty of lime juice, to taste.

4. Finely slice or chop the dried chilli and add that to the salsa, mixing well. (If using
fresh chillies, you can char these along with the other ingredients and remove the
skin when cool to chop.) The salsa will keep in the fridge for up to 3 days, but it's best
eaten on the day you make it.

Whipped Tomato Cream

200g (7oz) tomatoes
200ml (7fl oz) double (heavy) cream
¼ small bunch of herbs – any
combination (or individual) of tarragon
(especially nice), chervil, chives or
flat-leaf parsley, finely chopped

salt and freshly ground black pepper
¼ lemon
1–2 chive flowers (optional)

I came across this recipe for lightly whipped tomato cream in Richard Olney's Simple French Food. *A classic cookbook of its age, all elegant French cooking. This recipe was outstanding with cold roast chicken, but I can also imagine serving it alongside some simply cooked fish – sole or bream would be wonderful; or it would be very good alongside some scallops, on a blazing-hot summer's day, perhaps with some boiled green beans and new potatoes, also a glass of good dry white or rosé wine. This is broadly Olney's recipe, updated just a little with fresh herbs.*

1. Have a pan of water boiling. Slash the skin of each tomato with a sharp knife and plunge the tomatoes into the boiling water for 10 seconds. Remove with a slotted spoon and place the tomatoes under cold running water or into a bowl of ice-cold water for 30 seconds to arrest any further cooking. Remove from the cold water and the skins should then slip off easily. Finely dice the peeled tomato flesh, discarding any seeds and core.

2. Whip the cream to soft peaks, add the tomatoes and the herbs, seasoning well with salt, plenty of pepper and a little squeeze of lemon juice. Scatter over some chive flowers to finish, if you like. Serve immediately, or refrigerate for up to 1 hour – any longer and the whipped cream might collapse or begin to separate with the weight of the tomatoes.

Roasted Tomato Aïoli

100g (3½oz) tomatoes, halved
1 small garlic bulb, cloves separated,
  skin on
2 egg yolks
400ml (14fl oz) sunflower oil (or use
  100ml/3½fl oz) good olive oil and
  300ml/10½fl oz) sunflower oil), plus
  a splash for roasting

a splash of white wine or red wine
  vinegar, or more to taste (optional)
salt and freshly ground black pepper

This recipe is quite the opposite of the Whipped Tomato Cream (see page 37). A rich and glossy mayonnaise enriched with roasted tomatoes and a lot of garlic, it has a gorgeous pink hue in colour. I would suggest serving it with grilled or barbecued oily fish (mackerel or sardines, for example), also lamb chops, roast chicken or beef, or grilled steak. Endlessly versatile, it would also be good as a sandwich filling.

1. Preheat the oven to 180°C/160°C fan/350°F/Gas 4, and line a baking sheet with baking paper.

2. Place the tomato halves on the baking sheet and season them well with salt and pepper. Give them a splash of olive oil and add the garlic cloves to the tray. Roast for about 15-20 minutes, until the tomato halves and garlic cloves are soft. Remove from the oven and leave to cool a little before squeezing the garlic flesh from the skins into a bowl. Finely chop the roasted tomato halves, leaving behind any tough inner core, and put to one side.

3. In a bowl whisk the egg yolks with the roasted garlic flesh. Put the oil in a jug so that it is easy to pour, then slowly start whisking a few drops of oil into the egg and garlic mixture. Go very slowly to begin with, then gradually increase the quantity of oil you're adding each time, whisking in each addition so it is properly amalgamated, before adding the next.

4. Once the mayonnaise begins to hold its shape, you can start to add the oil in a thin, steady stream. When you have added all the oil, you should have a thick and wobbly mayonnaise that easily holds its shape.

5. Stir through the chopped roasted tomatoes and season well with salt and plenty of pepper - the aïoli should be highly seasoned. Add a splash of vinegar, if you like - you don't have to. Mix well. Covered, the aïoli will keep in the fridge for up to 3 days.

Quick Tomato and Chilli Chutney

MAKES 1 JAR
(ABOUT 450G/1LB)

2 tablespoons cooking oil, such as
   vegetable or sunflower
1 onion, finely chopped
1 teaspoon nigella seeds
1 teaspoon mustard seeds
1–3 teaspoons chilli flakes, according
   to taste

2 red chillies, finely chopped (deseeded
   if you want less heat)
400g (14oz) tomatoes, roughly chopped
½ teaspoon salt
2 tablespoons white wine vinegar or
   cider vinegar
1 tablespoon caster (superfine) sugar

A quick chutney to serve alongside a curry or anything fried, although also very good in a cheese sandwich. This recipe doesn't have the required levels of sugar, vinegar or salt to last indefinitely – it is more of a quick-style condiment to make and serve on the day, but it will last for up to a week if stored in the fridge. To be honest, though, it's not a gargantuan portion and my guess is that it will be spooned with a greedy gusto.

1. Heat the oil in a pan over a moderate heat. Add the onion, nigella seeds and mustard seeds and fry for about 5 minutes, until the onion has softened and the mustard seeds are beginning to pop.

2. Add the chilli flakes, fresh chillies, tomatoes, salt, vinegar, sugar and 100ml (3½fl oz) of water. Reduce the heat to medium–low and continue cooking for about 20 minutes, until the tomatoes have broken down and the sauce is thick and rich. Remove from the heat. Put the chutney in a bowl to serve just warm or cold, and generously. The chutney will store in the fridge for up to a week.

Chopped Small

Chopped small to scattergun over a dish, or eaten to wake up the tastebuds, giving juicy flavour and crunch to finish. What I want to show you here is that this family of condiments is a culinary format that is almost universal in context. Many countries serve a dish of chopped fresh ingredients supplemented with additional flavours as a condiment or small dish and, not surprisingly, given the subject matter of this cookbook, many of them contain tomatoes. These are by no means an exhaustive offering, just five of my most used combinations at home: an Indian chaat, a Mexican pico de gallo, a Middle Eastern-style chopped salad, a Spanish pipirrana and an Indonesian sambal colo-colo. All share a similar profile, offering sweet, sour, tangy, spicy and crunchy, and are all served as an appetizer or alongside another dish.

Chaat

1 cucumber, peeled, deseeded and finely diced
½ red onion, very finely diced
300g (10½oz) tomatoes, deseeded and finely diced
seeds from 1 small pomegranate; or use 1 small mango, peeled and diced
small bunch of coriander (cilantro), roughly chopped

1 x 400g (14oz) can of chickpeas, drained and rinsed
juice of ½ lemon
75g (2½oz) natural (plain) yogurt (optional)
1 green chilli, finely chopped (optional)
50g (1¾oz) Bombay mix or sev
2 teaspoons chaat masala
salt and freshly ground black pepper

1. Mix together the cucumber, onion, tomatoes, pomegranate seeds or mango, coriander, chickpeas and lemon juice, then season to taste with salt and pepper. Allow to rest for 15 minutes.

2. Put the mixture in a serving bowl or on a large platter and top with the yogurt and chilli (if using) and the Bombay mix and finally sprinkle with the chaat masala.

Pico de gallo

300g (10½oz) tomatoes, deseeded and finely diced
½ red onion, very finely diced
small bunch of coriander (cilantro), roughly chopped

2 garlic cloves, finely crushed
juice of 1 lime
about 1 jalapeño or green chilli, finely chopped, to taste

1. Mix all the ingredients together in a bowl. Leave them rest for 15 minutes, then serve.

Middle Eastern-style

300g (10½oz) tomatoes, deseeded and finely diced
½ red onion, very finely diced
1 garlic clove, finely crushed
1 green (bell) pepper, deseeded and very finely diced
1 cucumber, peeled, deseeded and finely diced

½ bunch of flat-leaf parsley, leaves picked and finely chopped
juice of ½ lemon, or extra to taste
3 tablespoons good olive oil
pinch of Aleppo or Urfa dried chilli flakes, or extra to taste
½–1 teaspoon sumac (optional)
pinch of dried mint or oregano
salt and freshly ground black pepper

1. Mix all the ingredients together in a bowl, adding extra acidity or spices to your liking, and season with salt and pepper. Leave to rest for 15 minutes, then serve.

Sambal colo-colo

300g (10½oz) tomatoes, deseeded and finely diced
½ red onion, very finely diced
1–3 red, finger-length chillies or bird's eye chillies, deseeded and sliced
4 tablespoons sweet Indonesian soy sauce (kecap manis)

juice of 1 juicy lime or 1 lemon
3 Thai basil sprigs, leaves picked and thinly sliced; or 3 coriander (cilantro) stems, leaves and tender stems picked and chopped

1. Combine all the ingredients together in a bowl. Leave them rest for 15 minutes, then serve.

Pipirrana

300g (10½oz) tomatoes, deseeded and finely diced
½ red onion, very finely diced
2 hard-boiled eggs, finely chopped
1 green (bell) pepper, deseeded and very finely chopped

½ cucumber, peeled, deseeded and finely chopped
2 tablespoons white wine vinegar
3 tablespoons good olive oil
salt and freshly ground black pepper

1. Combine all the ingredients together in a bowl and season with salt and pepper. Leave them rest for 15 minutes, then serve.

Tomatoes lend themselves perfectly well to soup-making, bringing flavour and velvety weight to the finished texture of so many different soups. And sure enough, there are a good many versions of tomato soup out there to choose from. For this chapter, I've listed some of my favourites – some with spices, some with herbs, whizzed, un-whizzed, some with bread as ballast, beans too, also yogurt and brown butter as a soothing slick. This was a hard list to whittle down to just eight recipes, and true to form, my recipe research and testing took me to many different countries. These tomato-based soups are all classics, some made with fresh tomatoes, some with canned. Your mood and the season you find yourself cooking in should help decide which soup to tackle and when.

Soups

Roasted Tomato and Yogurt Soup with Pine Nuts and Mint

800g (1lb 12oz) tomatoes, halved
1 onion, finely diced
3 garlic cloves, thinly sliced
60g (2oz) butter or ghee (or a sprinkle of olive oil)
75g (2½oz) short-grain, risotto or pudding rice
1 litre (35fl oz) chicken stock or water
1-2 teaspoons dried mint
1 tablespoon red chilli flakes, preferably Aleppo or Urfa

2 tablespoons pine nuts (or use crushed walnuts, or sunflower or pumpkin seeds)
juice of ½ lemon
1 tablespoon plain (all-purpose) flour
½ teaspoon salt, plus more to taste
1 egg, beaten
350g (12oz) full-fat natural (plain) yogurt
freshly ground black pepper

1. Preheat the oven to 220°C/200°C fan/425°F/Gas 7.

2. Arrange the tomatoes, cut-side up, in a roasting tin and add the onion. Stuff the sliced garlic deep down into the tomatoes, dot with half the butter or ghee (or use the olive oil) and season well with salt and pepper.

3. Roast the tomatoes for 15-20 minutes, until they are tender and beginning to caramelize at the edges. Remove from the oven, then blend three-quarters of them until smooth. Put both the blended and whole baked tomatoes to one side.

4. While the tomatoes are roasting, put the rice and the chicken stock or water together into a pan and bring to a boil over a high heat. Place a lid on the pan and reduce the heat to simmer with the lid on for about 20-30 minutes, until the rice is tender and cooked through. Give the rice a good stir every now and then. Remove from the heat and keep warm.

5. While the rice is cooking, in a small pan heat the remaining butter or ghee (or oil) along with the dried mint and chilli flakes for 1-2 minutes, until just beginning to bubble, then stir in the pine nuts (or alternatives) and lemon juice. Remove from the heat and put to one side.

6. In a bowl, whisk together the flour, salt, egg and yogurt.

7. Whisk the yogurt mixture into the cooked, soupy rice, stirring well, then gently heat, never boiling, for about 5 minutes for the egg to cook out and the soup to take on a creamy, homogenous liquid consistency. Add the blended tomatoes, stirring to heat through. Check the seasoning, adding more salt and pepper, as necessary.

8. To serve, ladle the soup into bowls, distribute the remaining roasted tomatoes among the bowls and spoon over the spiced butter. Serve hot.

Stabilizing and thickening a soup using a mixture of egg and plain yogurt and a scant spoon of flour is a Turkish preparation I have enjoyed both in northern Cyprus and in London's Turkish restaurants. It's the sort of gentle alchemy that I like and admire in Turkish cooking. In this soup, a small amount of rice provides bulk. The spiced butter serves to remind us all that, while warm, soupy bowls of delicious-flavoured ingredients are comforting and lifegiving, what we all need, almost always, is a good slick of spiced molten butter spiked with invigorating dried mint. I cannot imagine many things that this spiced butter will not make taste better – a few, but not many.

Gazpacho

1 red (bell) pepper, deseeded and
    finely chopped
1 small green (bell) pepper, deseeded
    and finely chopped
1 cucumber, peeled, deseeded and
    finely chopped
1kg (2lb 4oz) tomatoes, roughly
    chopped
2 garlic cloves, finely chopped

½–1 teaspoon salt, to taste
100g (3½oz) crustless dry bread
    (ciabatta is good), broken into
    little pieces
150ml (5fl oz) good olive oil,
    plus more to serve
2 teaspoons red wine vinegar,
    or more to taste
a pinch of sugar, to taste

Some chefs and cooks will vouch for a super-smooth gazpacho; others insist on serving this soup with a little more texture, blended, pounded or otherwise. As for serving suggestions, these tend to get even more varied than the making of this famous Andalusian soup itself. I've seen ice cubes added; croûtons added; a trio of tomatoes, cucumber and pepper diced so small and uniform; the soup in miniature served as an eye-catching, crunchy garnish. I've seen it ladled into bowls, into glasses, even served in shot glasses to jumpstart the appetite. As with all recipes, there are many ways to riff. This is a framework for you to work from. Tasting throughout the making of gazpacho is paramount, because balance is all. You may need to add a touch more sweetness or acidity or salt, depending on the raw ingredients you are working with at the time. One thing is for sure, good olive oil is crucial – a viscous slick of green on all that red.

1. Reserve about 2 tablespoons each of the chopped peppers and the cucumber to garnish the gazpacho when you come to serve it, if you like.

2. Mix the remaining peppers and cucumber with the tomatoes, garlic and salt and allow to macerate at room temperature for at least 30 minutes, although a couple of hours is good.

3. Soak the bread in a little cold water for about 5 minutes, then squeeze it out. Place in a bowl and stir in half the olive oil and all of the vinegar, then put it to one side.

4. Blend the vegetables until completely smooth, adding more salt to taste, if you like. You can then push this mixture through a fine sieve if you want a super-smooth texture – I rarely bother. Add the soaked bread and blend until completely smooth.

5. With the motor running, add the remaining oil in a thin stream, to emulsify.

6. Chill completely, then check the seasoning before serving, adding more salt and vinegar to taste, and perhaps a pinch of sugar, too.

7. Ladle the gazpacho into bowls and garnish with the reserved finely chopped pepper and cucumber and a drizzle more of olive oil. If you want some additional toppings, try shredded jamón, best-quality, sustainable canned tuna, fried croûtons, chopped olives or chopped hard-boiled egg.

Pappa al Pomodoro

2 or 3 garlic cloves, very thinly sliced
100ml (3½fl oz) good olive oil, plus more
   to serve
2 x 400g (14oz) cans of whole plum
   tomatoes, drained of juice; or use fresh
   and peeled (see page 37)

about 200g (7oz) stale good-quality
   bread, such as ciabatta, crusts cut off
   and torn into smaller pieces
a small bunch of basil, leaves picked and
   bigger leaves torn into smaller pieces
salt and freshly ground black pepper

Perfection. Use peeled, ripe tomatoes or good-quality canned, drained of juice. This is an Italian recipe and one that, for me, symbolizes why Italian cooking is such a powerhouse when it comes to good food. With few ingredients, the emphasis here, and indeed with so much Italian cookery, rests on quality and sensitive cookery practice. Tomatoes, garlic, basil, good bread, good olive oil, salt and pepper – that's it. Served warm, never piping hot, this soft, luscious and soothing soup is one of my favourites.

1. Put the garlic and half the olive oil in a saucepan over a moderate heat. Cook gently for 1 minute, until the garlic is fragrant but not at all coloured.

2. Add the tomatoes and cook gently over a low heat for about 30 minutes to concentrate the tomatoes, stirring every now and then. Season the tomatoes with salt and pepper and add 500ml (17fl oz) of cold water to the pan.

3. Bring the mixture to a boil and add the bread. Stir well so that the bread absorbs all the liquid. Add a splash more water if the soup is too thick, although remember you want this soup to be quite dense.

4. Remove the pan from the heat and add the basil and remaining olive oil, stirring well and checking the seasoning – adjust with more salt and pepper, if necessary. Set the pan to one side in order for the soup to cool a little.

5. Serve just warm, never piping hot, with extra olive oil at the table, if you wish.

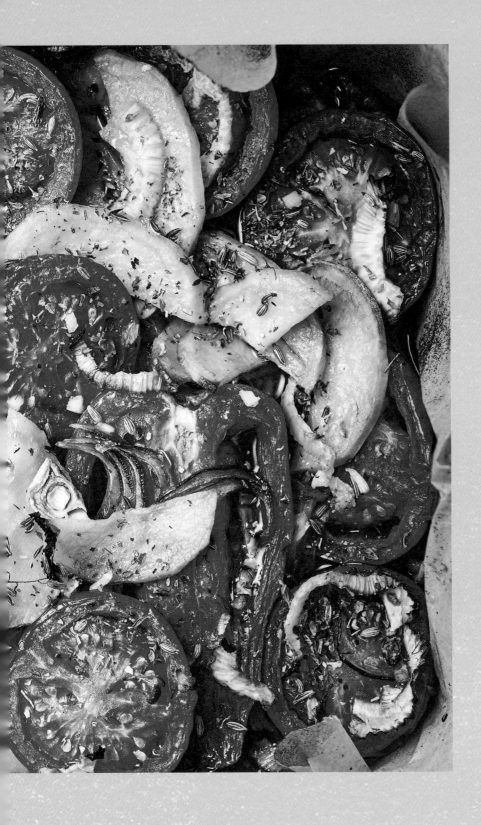

Rasam

**For the rasam powder
(makes 100g/3½oz)**
80g (2¾oz) red lentils
10 dried red chillies
10 curry leaves, fresh or frozen
3 tablespoons coriander seeds
1 tablespoon cumin seeds
1 teaspoon black peppercorns
1 teaspoon asafoetida
1 heaped teaspoon ground turmeric
about 1 teaspoon jaggery or palm sugar

For the soup
50g (1¾oz) red lentils
3 large tomatoes, fresh or drained
  canned, finely chopped

1 teaspoon ground turmeric
½ teaspoon chilli powder
½ teaspoon salt, plus more to taste
2 tablespoons ghee or oil, or a knob
  of butter
1 teaspoon cumin seeds
½ teaspoon mustard seeds
10 curry leaves, fresh or frozen
2 tablespoons tamarind paste
a big pinch of asafoetida or ground
  fenugreek
1 tablespoon homemade rasam powder,
  plus more to taste
freshly ground black pepper
½ small bunch of coriander (cilantro),
  finely chopped, to serve

This is a hot-and-sour soup served in southern India with rice or roti for a simple meal, or on its own as an appetizer to rouse the tastebuds. During my trip through the southern states of India, we would often stop and have a thali for lunch, usually served on tin platters and including rasam – a thin, watery soup, contrasting in texture to the various dahl and curries. Best of all was dunking the roti in the rasam, leaving it to soak up the spiced tomato juices before popping it in my mouth. The blend of spices used in this, my recipe for rasam, really ramp up the flavour. Use ghee to fry off some mustard seeds, then throw this over the finished soup to serve, a bubbling slick of scented, spiced butter.

Crucial to this soup is the pre-made rasam powder, which you add at the end of the cooking time to thicken and flavour. You can buy a ready-made rasam blend, but it is relatively quick and easy to make at home. Stored in an airtight container, it keeps well.

1. First, make the rasam powder. In a dry pan over a moderate heat, toast the lentils for about 3-5 minutes, until bronzed. Remove them from the pan and put to one side. Toast the chillies for about 2-3 minutes in the same pan, until fragrant, then put to one side. Toast the curry leaves for about 2-3 minutes, until crisp, and put to one side. Toast the coriander and cumin seeds until they smoke and crackle (30-60 seconds), put to one side, then finally do the same with the peppercorns. Use a good blender to process all the toasted ingredients, along with the asafoetida, turmeric and jaggery or palm sugar, to form a fine powder. Store in a sealed jar. The mixture will last indefinitely but is best when it's fresh – within 2 weeks of toasting and grinding.

2. Make the soup. Put the lentils in a pan with 600ml (21fl oz) of water, half of the chopped tomatoes, and the turmeric, chilli powder and salt. Place over a high heat and bring to a boil. Then, reduce the heat to a simmer, cover the pan and cook for about 30 minutes, until deeply aromatic and the lentils are completely collapsed.

3. Meanwhile heat the ghee or oil in a small pan over a high heat. Add the cumin seeds and mustard seeds and fry for a minute or two, until they begin to splutter, then add the curry leaves and cook for 10 seconds more. Add the remaining tomatoes, and the tamarind, the asafoetida or fenugreek and the rasam powder.

4. Bring to a boil, simmer for 5 minutes, then add the mixture to the pan with the cooked lentils.

5. Check for seasoning and add more salt, pepper and rasam powder, if required. You can also add a little more water if you like, depending on how lose you want to serve the rasam. Add the coriander (cilantro), to serve.

Roasted Tomato, Fennel and Potato Soup with Fried Sourdough, Pumpkin Seeds and Halloumi

1.2kg (2lb 12oz) tomatoes, halved (unless small)
250g (9oz) waxy potatoes, peeled and sliced
1 red onion, thinly sliced into rings
1 teaspoon ground fennel
4–6 garlic cloves, skin on
about 3 good-sized thyme sprigs, leaves picked
6 tablespoons olive oil, plus more to serve

2 thick slices of sourdough, or similar rustic loaf, cut into 2cm (¾in) cubes (crusts on is fine)
600–800ml (21–28fl oz) chicken or vegetable stock, or use water
50g (1¾oz) pumpkin seeds
100g (3½oz) halloumi, drained and cut into 2cm (¾in) cubes
a good pinch of chilli flakes, to taste
salt and freshly ground black pepper

Blended super-smooth, the tomatoes are impossibly rich and glossy in this soup, blitzed as they are with the fennel and potato. Roasting the tomatoes intensifies their flavour, likewise the fennel. Fennel is part of the parsley family and shares that same anise-type characteristic, which pairs so beautifully with tomato – boosting sweetly fragrant notes in the soup, liquorice-like, and ultimately flattering the tomatoes no end. As for the scattergun of toppings, these are by no means set in stone. I'm just suggesting this combination works well with this soup. Switch to feta if you prefer, or leave out dairy entirely; likewise, the croûtons, and do use whichever seeds or nuts you have to hand.

1. Preheat the oven to 200°C/180°C fan/400°F/Gas 6. Spread the tomatoes, cut side up, and the potato slices on a baking sheet lined with baking paper. Add the onion, ground fennel and garlic. Add two-thirds of the thyme leaves and drizzle with half the olive oil. Roast for 25–30 minutes, until the veg is tender, the garlic soft, and the tomatoes have just begun to caramelize. Leave to cool for 5 minutes.

2. Meanwhile, put the pieces of bread on a separate baking sheet and drizzle with 1 tablespoon of the remaining olive oil. Roast for about 10 minutes, turning the bread midway through the cooking time, until golden brown and crunchy. Remove the croûtons from the oven and set to one side.

3. When the roasted vegetables are cool enough to process, blend them with their cooking juices in a food processor or blender until creamy and smooth. Place the soup in a saucepan over a low heat, add the stock to your preferred thickness, then stir and add salt and pepper to taste. Bring to a gentle simmer, then remove from the heat.

4. While the soup is heating up, add another tablespoon of the remaining olive oil and the pumpkin seeds to a frying pan over a moderate heat and fry the seeds for about 3 minutes, until they pop and sizzle. Remove from the heat and put to one side.

5. Wipe out the pan and add the remaining tablespoon of olive oil. Place the pan back over a moderate heat and fry the halloumi for about 2 minutes, turning frequently, until the cubes are golden all over. Add the remaining thyme leaves, along with the fried pumpkin seeds, chilli flakes and croûtons. Put to one side in a serving bowl.

6. Top the soup with the croûton mixture and serve with an extra slick of olive oil.

Fisherman's Soup

4 tablespoons olive oil

1 small onion, finely diced or sliced

3 celery sticks, finely diced or sliced

3 garlic cloves, finely sliced

pinch of chilli flakes, or use sliced green or red chilli

5 plum tomatoes, diced small, or 1 x 400g (14oz) can of plum tomatoes, drained and diced

600ml (21fl oz) fish or vegetable stock

100ml (3½fl oz) white wine or additional fish or vegetable stock

500g (1lb 2oz) firm, white sustainable fish fillet, cut into 2–3cm (¾–1¼in) pieces

200g (7oz) peeled, raw prawns (shrimp) or 500g (1lb 2oz) clams or mussels

juice of ½ lemon, small orange or lime

salt and freshly ground black pepper

½ small bunch of flat-leaf parsley, dill, tarragon, coriander (cilantro) or basil, leaves picked and finely chopped, to serve

So-called because this soup was known to be a working man's dish – made by fishermen, or those involved in fishing, with scraps of freshly caught fish too small or inferior to sell to market. With pretty much all fish now at an all-time premium, and likely to be forever more, I think this is a useful recipe to reinterpret for the modern day – it extends a small portion of fish to feed more people. Poaching the fish in this tomato-laced broth, then adding mussels, clams or prawns, unlocks unparalleled flavour. It is a joyful dish to serve among friends, and fishermen or fisherwomen or otherwise. The fish you use, likewise your choice of herbs, chilli and citrus, might go some way to determining on what beach in the world you might be cooking your catch. It goes without saying, buy sustainably caught fish, from sustainable stocks and from a reputable fishmonger or supplier.

1. Heat 3 tablespoons of the olive oil in a wide, shallow saucepan over a moderate–low heat, then add the onion and celery, cooking for about 8–10 minutes, until soft but not coloured. Add the garlic and chilli flakes or sliced chilli and cook for 2 minutes more.

2. Add the chopped tomatoes, seasoning well with salt and pepper, and turn up the heat to moderate, then continue cooking for another 3–5 minutes, until rich and thickened.

3. Pour in the stock and wine or additional stock, bringing the pan to a quick boil over a high heat. Add the fish fillet, turn down to moderate again so that the liquid starts to simmer, cover with a lid and simmer until the fish is opaque and just cooked through – about 5–7 minutes, depending on the size and thickness of the fish. Add the shellfish for the final 2 minutes of the cooking time, cooking until the mussels or clams have opened (discard any that don't) or the prawns have turned opaque.

4. Check the seasoning, adding more salt and pepper, if necessary, then add the citrus juice and remove the pan from the heat.

5. To serve, divide the soup between the bowls and scatter with the herbs, adding a slick of olive oil to each serving.

TIP: To make a quick fish stock, put about 400g (14oz) fish bones and/or prawn shells (if you have them from the prawns) in a saucepan with a peeled garlic clove, a couple of parsley stalks and a few slices of celery and onion. Cover with 800ml (28fl oz) of cold water, bring the liquid to a boil and skim off any froth that collects. Simmer for about 10 minutes. Strain and put to one side until ready to use.

Hot, Sour and Fragrant Soup
with Tomatoes and Chicken

1.2 litres (40fl oz) chicken stock
4 lime leaves, thinly sliced
2–3 lemongrass stalks, each cut
   into 3 pieces
3–6 bird's eye red or green chillies,
   ½ thinly sliced, ½ left whole
4 thin slices of fresh galangal or ginger
   (unpeeled is fine)
½ small bunch of coriander (cilantro),
   leaves and stalks separated

300g (10½oz) cherry tomatoes, halved
2 very thin slices of unwaxed lime
1 large boneless chicken breast or leg,
   or use 2 large thighs (about 200g/7oz),
   cut into 2cm (¾in) dice
100g (3½oz) small mushrooms, sliced
   1cm (½in) thick
juice of 2 limes
2 tablespoons Thai fish sauce, plus more
   to taste

Thai soups are often served as a supplement to the main course, never as a precursor. They are enjoyed as a means to refresh and also cleanse. This is a seasoned broth and intensely fragrant. I've included tomatoes because their fruity, sweet, acidic flavour complements the lime leaves, lemongrass and coriander, all equally highly perfumed. Here, I've made the soup with chicken stock and diced chicken, but you could also use fish or vegetable stock, and switch to prawns (shrimp) or firm tofu, if you prefer. A fairly simple assembly, balance is all – hot, sour, fragrant.

1. Heat the stock to boiling point in a saucepan over a high heat.

2. Bruise the lime leaves, lemongrass, whole chillies, galangal or ginger and coriander stalks in a pestle and mortar. (Alternatively, use a bowl and the end of a rolling pin or briefly pulse in a food processor.)

3. Add this mixture along with the tomatoes and lime slices to the boiling stock, turn down the heat and simmer for 5 minutes.

4. Add the chicken and the mushrooms and simmer for about 5–8 minutes, until the chicken is cooked through.

5. Remove the pan from the heat and immediately add the sliced chillies, lime juice, fish sauce and coriander leaves, all to taste, then serve.

Tomato, Chipotle Chilli and Oregano Soup with Feta and Black Beans

4 tablespoons olive oil
2 onions, finely chopped
2 celery sticks, finely diced
½ teaspoon salt
7 garlic cloves, finely chopped
2 tablespoons chipotle in adobo,
   finely chopped (or use chipotle paste
   or 1 teaspoon smoked paprika and chilli
   powder or flakes, to taste)
2 tablespoon tomato purée
   (concentrated paste)
400g (14oz) tomatoes, peeled, or
   1 x 400g (14oz) can of plum tomatoes
3 bay leaves, scrunched a little
1 x 400g (14oz) can of black beans,
   drained and rinsed

800ml (28fl oz) chicken stock or water,
   plus extra if needed
salt and freshly ground black pepper

To serve
1 avocado, peeled, stoned and diced
100g (3½oz) sour cream
100g (3½oz) feta, crumbled
½ small bunch of coriander (cilantro),
   roughly chopped
80g (2¾oz) corn tortilla chips, crushed
1-2 chillies (habanero or jalapeño are
   ideal), thinly sliced
hot sauce of choice (see page 25 to make
   your own)
1 lime, cut into wedges

If you have the time and inclination, it's worth soaking and cooking your own black beans for this recipe. However, you can make it just as well with a can of black beans and some stock. Adding tomatoes to this bean soup brings a velvety, fruity acidity to the creamy weight of black beans. My serving suggestion is quite lengthy, but in my mind absolutely worth it. The soup would go especially well with a dollop of hot sauce to serve (see page 25).

1. Heat the oil in a saucepan over a moderate heat. Add the onions, celery and salt and cook for about 10-12 minutes, until the onions are soft and just beginning to brown. Add the garlic and cook for 2 minutes more, to soften.

2. Add the chipotles (plus any liquid), the tomato purée, tomatoes and bay leaves and cook for 10-15 minutes, until rich and thick.

3. Add the beans and stock and bring the liquid to a boil. You can add a splash more stock if you think it needs it, depending on how thick you'd like the soup to be when you come to serve it. Check the seasoning, adding salt and pepper, as necessary.

4. Remove the soup from the heat. I like to partially blend the soup at this point – about one third blended is ideal. Remove the bay leaves, then use a stick blender in the pan or remove a portion and blend that before adding it back to the pan.

5. Serve the warm soup in bowls and top each bowl with chopped avocado, sour cream, feta, coriander, corn chips and chillies, and with hot sauce and lime wedges for helping yourselves.

Perhaps the most straightforward of all the chapters in this cookbook to write and to recipe test - salads are exactly what tomatoes are meant for. Tomatoes bring so many different qualities to so many styles of salad - some thrown together with a casual insouciance that makes creating good food look entirely effortless, and some a little more composed... the tomatoes, ultimately, ending up as a stunning work of art.

As with all the recipes in this book, I am cooking with a global outlook. For this chapter, through the prism of raw tomatoes, I concentrate on local cuisines that revere and celebrate tomatoes, and also perhaps that encourage salads as main courses or as great big dishes to bring to the table, buffet-style, where many plates of food create the one meal.

There are just eight recipes here, so make them all, and do feel free to use them as a blueprint to then riff from - if not peaches, use plums, melon or apricots; experiment using alternative favourite herbs, or those you have to hand; add chopped grapes, plums, watermelon or pomegranate seeds to the tabbouleh, even. These are recipes, not doctrines - food is, after all, a fairly flexible medium, and the recipes are here to encourage, not intimidate.

One last thing to say: the composition of a salad is one of my favourite kitchen tasks, paying attention to balance in the finished dish - for how attractive the salad looks when you come to plate it, of course, but also when you come to eat it, ensuring that each portion is replete with additional ingredients and that each mouthful is dressed exactly so. Salads are the most perfect of meals to eat outdoors, so seize the day, sunshine or clouds, and always, always use perfectly ripe tomatoes.

Salads

Tomatoes with Peaches, Grapes, Feta and Oregano

4 tablespoons good olive oil

1 tablespoon red or white wine vinegar or cider vinegar

½ small red onion or 1 shallot, very thinly sliced

2 peaches, stoned and diced into 2–3cm (¾–1¼in) pieces

600g (1lb 5oz) tomatoes (mixed colours and sizes is nice), diced into 2–3cm (¾–1¼in) pieces

200g (7oz) red grapes, halved

½ small bunch of oregano or marjoram, leaves picked

50g (1¾oz) feta, crumbled

50g (1¾oz) kalamata olives, pitted and roughly chopped

salt and freshly ground black pepper

Choose multi-coloured tomatoes, as well as yellow or white-fleshed peaches, and purple, black or green grapes. Dice the fruit so that they are all roughly uniform in size, and be sure to taste and dress the salad accordingly. Use soft goat's cheese, if you prefer, although Roquefort or mozzarella would also work beautifully. The sweet juicy fruits flattering the salty cheese and black olives is crucial for the balance in this recipe.

1. In a small bowl mix together the oil and vinegar and add the onion, seasoning with salt and pepper to taste. Put to one side to macerate for 10 minutes.

2. Put the peaches, tomatoes and grapes into a large serving bowl.

3. Add the oregano or marjoram, the feta and the olives and spoon over the dressing. Serve immediately.

Panzanella

1 large red (bell) pepper, deseeded and cut lengthways into 4 broad slices

1 large yellow (bell) pepper, deseeded and cut lengthways into 4 broad slices

2 red chillies (not too hot; deseeded if you want less heat)

600g (1lb 5oz) tomatoes, roughly chopped into 2–3cm (¾–1¼in) pieces

1 small red onion, very thinly sliced

1 tablespoon capers

30g (1oz) best-quality black olives, pitted and roughly chopped

2–4 salted anchovies, finely chopped, to taste (optional)

200g (7oz) day-old good-quality bread (such as sourdough or ciabatta), roughly torn into 2–3cm (¾–1¼in) pieces

a good pinch of salt, plus more to season

1 small garlic clove, crushed

3 tablespoons red wine vinegar

6 tablespoons good olive oil

a small bunch of basil, leaves picked and torn

freshly ground black pepper

I have been served panzanella salads that are overwrought and deconstructed, with each ingredient alone and standing proud of each other on a plate. They are absolutely not what a panzanella should be. Rather, this is an Italian bread salad that combines tomatoes, peppers, capers, olives, anchovies and onions to form a soft and luscious jumble. The basil most certainly loses its lustre and looks, but gives off a vaunted, heady scent. Crucially, the salad must then be left to sit and wallow, the bread soaking up the tomato juices, vinegar and olive oil, turning tender, even a little wobbly, and so far removed from bread, the ingredient goes on to become entirely something new and of itself. The tomato juices are key to this recipe, the bread must sit and soak in them, so be sure to collect them as you chop.

1. Get the grill (broiler) hot. Grill the pepper slices, skin side up, and the whole chillies under a fierce heat, until the skins blister and blacken. Remove from the heat and put into a sealed container (this will help when you come to peel them). Set to one side to cool. Once cool, peel the skins – they should slip off – and discard them. Roughly chop the pepper flesh and finely chop the chillies, seeds and all.

2. Put the grilled peppers and chillies with the tomatoes, onion, capers, olives and anchovies in a large bowl, mixing well to combine.

3. Add the bread and salt and let the salad sit in the bowl at room temperature for about 30 minutes for the juices to run and the flavours to meld.

4. In a small bowl, mix together the garlic, vinegar and oil, seasoning well with salt and plenty of freshly ground black pepper.

5. When you're ready to serve, add the dressing along with the torn basil leaves, mixing well to combine. Serve immediately.

SALADS

Niçoise

3 eggs

800g (1lb 12oz) tomatoes, cut into wedges

300g (10½oz) new potatoes, peeled and cut into 3cm (1¼in) pieces

300g (10½oz) runner, flat or French beans, cut into 5cm (2in) lengths

2 shallots or 1 small red onion, very thinly sliced

80g (2¾oz) best-quality black olives, pitted

2 tablespoons capers

10 anchovies in oil, drained and halved, to taste (optional)

½ bunch of basil or flat-leaf parsley, leaves picked and roughly chopped

For the dressing

1 tablespoon Dijon mustard

2 tablespoons red wine vinegar

6 tablespoons good olive oil

1 garlic clove, crushed

big pinch of salt

freshly ground black pepper

Truthfully, we should all avoid eating tuna. The data points to a marine species in a catastrophic state of collapse, with only line-caught albacore from the Atlantic listed by the Marine Conservation Society as an acceptable option – all other tuna are best avoided. So, my suggestion here is to make a niçoise salad minus tuna and use instead fat, luscious fingers of salted anchovy.

Without wanting to come across as too bossy or doom-mongering, I think we should also exercise caution when it comes to eating anchovies. Bay of Biscay anchovies are known as foraging species that exist along with smaller sea life at the bottom of the marine food chain. This means that they currently have the green light to eat as a sustainable source.

Now, on to matters niçoise – one of my favourite all-time salads. Tomatoes and one of their best friends, anchovies, are showcased here to dizzying effect along with hard-boiled eggs, cooked green beans, olives, capers and more. I am a child of the 1990s and it was my mum's salad niçoise, made with iceberg lettuce and black olives from a can, that heralded summer (salad for supper!), making me feel more sophisticated than my 10-year-old self ever thought possible. My mum would assemble the salad; meanwhile I was allowed to whisk together a French vinaigrette – heavy on the Dijon, a raw clove of garlic, a glossy, golden emulsion, blissful is the memory. I can still taste it.

1. Put the eggs in a pan of cold water and bring them slowly to a boil. Simmer for 8 minutes, then drain and plunge them into cold water. Leave them until they are cool enough to peel, then put them to one side.

2. Make the dressing. Mix together the Dijon and red wine vinegar in a small bowl. Gradually whisk in the oil to form a thick dressing. Add the garlic, salt and a good amount of freshly ground black pepper, and put to one side.

3. In a large serving bowl, season the tomatoes well with salt and freshly ground black pepper - this will help the juices run. Put to one side.

4. Boil the potatoes in plenty of well-salted water for about 15 minutes, or until tender, adding the beans for the final 3–5 minutes (depending on the variety). Remove from the heat, drain well and tip them back into the pan.

5. Add the shallots or onion to the drained potatoes and green beans and dress them with the salad dressing while still warm.

6. Add the potato and bean mixture to the tomatoes in the bowl. Add the olives, capers and anchovies, mixing well to combine. Halve or quarter the boiled eggs and dot them over the top of the salad, then scatter over the basil or parsley and serve.

Plate of Tomatoes with Hard-boiled Eggs, Pickles and Za'atar

4 eggs
olive oil
250g (9oz) halloumi, cut into 4 thick
  slices
400g (14oz) tomatoes, sliced
200g (7oz) hummus
50g (1¾oz) best-quality black or green
  olives, pitted

1 cucumber, peeled if it has a tough skin,
  and cut into 5mm (¼in) slices
shop-bought pickles
2 tablespoons za'atar
flaky sea salt
pita bread, warmed, to serve

This is exactly the sort of breakfast I love to eat most of all. Tomatoes make up the mainstay here, seasoned with flaky salt and a good slick of olive oil, they really complement and showcase the other ingredients – the salty halloumi and olives, the dense, buttery hard-boiled eggs, the hummus (shop-bought or make your own), the clean and crunchy cucumber, the pickles and the winning blend of spice and seeds that is za'atar. You could stuff it all in the warm pita and eat it as a sandwich, but I prefer to tear off pieces of pita, taking care each time to fastidiously assemble the perfect mouthful. For breakfast (as this might be served in some warmer Mediterranean countries) with strong coffee it's wonderful, but honestly, this is anytime-of-the-day eating. Enjoy.

1. Put the eggs in a pan of cold water and bring them slowly to a boil. Simmer for 8 minutes, then drain and put them into cold water to stop them cooking. Peel them after about 10 minutes and then slice them.

2. Heat a splash of oil in a pan over a moderate heat. Add the halloumi and fry for 1–2 minutes, until the underside of each slice is golden brown. Flip the slices and cook on the other side. Work in batches, if you need to – don't overcrowd the pan. Put to one side and keep warm.

3. On a large serving plate, arrange the tomatoes and season well with flaky salt and olive oil. Add the cooked halloumi slices, hard-boiled eggs and hummus. Then, add the olives, cucumber and pickles.

4. Scatter the plate with the za'atar, or place it in a contained pile on the plate so you can season as you eat.

5. Serve with warmed pita breads and extra olive oil to sprinkle as you eat.

Carpaccio of Tomatoes with Tapenade

For the carpaccio

1 small fennel bulb, trimmed and very thinly sliced or shaved

salt

2 tablespoons Chardonnay or muscatel vinegar (or use white wine vinegar sweetened with a pinch of sugar)

800g (1lb 12oz) tomatoes, mixed colours and sizes, very thinly sliced

4 tablespoons good olive oil

20g (¾oz) rocket (arugula), washed and dried

For the tapenade

100g (3½oz) best-quality kalamata olives, pitted

1 thyme sprig, leaves picked

1 garlic clove, crushed

1 tablespoon capers, desalinated and drained, or use pickled

6 anchovy fillets (optional, but sort of non-negotiable when it comes to tapenade)

4 tablespoons good olive oil

salt and freshly ground black pepper

Usually meant for meat or fish, carpaccio as a method for preparing tomatoes serves them very well indeed. It goes without saying, a sharp knife is essential. Slice the tomatoes very thinly and do try to keep them in form. A mixture of shape and colour is ideal here – laying them out attractively on a plate is the kind of meditative kitchen task that I find particularly enjoyable. If ever there were a time to really knuckle down and, as they say in the industry, plate something, then this is just that. Tomatoes as a work of art, with the inky black tapenade a fitting signature.

1. Toss the fennel with a pinch of salt and the vinegar and put to one side.

2. Make the tapenade. Put the olives, thyme, garlic, capers and anchovies on a board and chop, or pulse in a processor, until you have a coarse paste. Mix in the olive oil and season to taste with salt and pepper.

3. Lay the tomatoes out over a platter or large plate, seasoning each layer with pepper and a pinch of salt (remembering the tapenade is salty). Drizzle with the olive oil and allow to rest for 5 minutes.

4. To serve, add the fennel and rocket and spoon the tapenade over.

Tomato, Corn and Jalapeño with Feta, Coriander and Lime

4 corn-on-the-cobs
a bunch of spring onions (scallions), trimmed
250g (9oz) tomatoes, finely chopped
1 red (bell) pepper, deseeded and finely diced
1 avocado, stoned, peeled and finely chopped
1–2 jalapeño chillies, finely chopped (or use another green chilli)
a small bunch of coriander (cilantro), roughly chopped
75g (2½oz) queso fresco or feta, crumbled
juice of about 2 limes, to taste
salt and freshly ground black pepper

Chargrilling the corn-on-the-cobs is the only real cooking you will have to do for this recipe. Jalapeño chillies are pretty widespread to buy these days – it's worth searching out specific chillies for a recipe when specified, as chillies can vary widely in profile. Jalapeños have a juicy, grassy flavour and are usually not all that hot, which means that you can slice a good few, as in this recipe, and not have to feel too terrified. I'd love for you to use a Mexican queso fresco as the cheese. If you don't have access to it, use feta instead – dry, salty and crumbly it will do a similar job. Alternatively, omit the cheese entirely to keep things vegan. Scrunching up a bag of corn tortilla chips to add to the salad gives an unbeatable texture to the end result.

1. Grill the corn over a high heat for about 6–8 minutes, turning to cook and colour each side and until tender. (Alternatively, boil the corns for about 5 minutes, if you prefer.)

2. While the corn is cooking, grill the spring onions for 1–2 minutes on each side, until nicely coloured. (Alternatively, thinly slice them and use them raw.)

3. Put the cobs and spring onions on a plate to cool. Once cool enough to handle, slice the corn kernels off the cobs and roughly chop the spring onions, then put them in a large serving bowl.

4. Stir in the remaining ingredients, adding lime juice and seasoning with salt and pepper to taste. Mix well.

Tabbouleh with Tomatoes, Plums and Plenty of Mint

60g (2oz) coarse bulgur wheat

2–3 plums, stoned and diced very small

1–2 spring onions (scallions), thinly sliced, to taste

500g (1lb 2oz) tomatoes, peeled, halved and diced very small, juices reserved

juice of ½–1 lemon

2–3 tablespoons good olive oil

1 small garlic clove, crushed to a paste with a little salt

½ teaspoon baharat spice blend or ground cinnamon

2 teaspoons sumac (optional, but thoroughly recommended)

large bunch of flat-leaf parsley, leaves picked and roughly chopped

large bunch of mint, leaves picked and roughly chopped

salt and freshly ground black pepper

It's not uncommon to find tabbouleh served as a dreary tumble of ingredients. My advice is, first, use as many herbs as you can bother to chop finely, then look for added magic – in this recipe, not just tomatoes (of course), but also ripe and juicy plums, one of my favourite stone fruits. Plums come into season just as tomatoes bid farewell to their time to shine, making this a perfect match. Chop them small and delight in a mixture that is anything but dreary – both the plums and the tomatoes blush the soaked bulgur a rather beautiful shade of pink.

1. Soak the bulgur wheat in 120ml (4fl oz) of warm water for 30 minutes, or until the grains are tender and all the water has been absorbed. Drain any excess water away.

2. In a large mixing bowl, combine the plums and spring onions with the tomatoes, tomato juices and cooked bulgur and mix well to combine.

3. In a small bowl, make a dressing by whisking together the lemon juice, oil, garlic, baharat and sumac. Season well with salt and plenty of pepper.

4. Dress the tomatoes, plums, spring onions and bulgur with the dressing and finally add the herbs, mixing well to combine. Serve.

Cherry Tomatoes and Green Beans with Bird's Eye Chilli, Lime and Peanuts

1–2 garlic cloves, peeled

1–2 bird's eye chillies, thinly sliced

1 tablespoon palm sugar or use light brown sugar

juice of 2 limes, and to taste

1 tablespoon Thai fish sauce, and to taste

300g (10½oz) cherry tomatoes, halved

300g (10½oz) long beans (such as green beans, French beans or romano/ flat beans), trimmed and cut into 3cm (1¼in) lengths

1 cucumber, peeled, cored and chopped into 3cm (1¼in) lengths

½ small bunch of Thai basil or mint, leaves picked and roughly chopped

60g (2oz) roasted salted peanuts, roughly crushed

50g (1¾oz) shop-bought crispy fried shallots (optional)

Ideally, you will have a good-sized pestle and mortar for this recipe. But, if not, never fear – use instead a sturdy mixing bowl and the bottom of a rolling pin. You want to give both the tomatoes and green beans a good bashing, denting the flesh to soften and release any juices into the bowl; the dented green beans then drinking in the dressing. Bird's eye chilli – you have been warned, go big and be bold; and with lime and lots of crushed peanuts, this is a most delicious summer side salad.

1. Using a mortar and pestle, pound the garlic, chilli and sugar together. Add the lime juice and fish sauce and season to taste with more or less lime juice and fish sauce to your liking. Alternatively, whizz the lot in a mini food processor to form a dressing.

2. Put the tomatoes and green beans in a bowl and bruise the lot with the pestle, or use a rolling pin. Add the cucumber and the dressing to the bowl. Toss, then let the salad sit for 10 minutes for the flavours to meld and the juices to run.

3. Add the Thai basil or mint, peanuts, and crispy shallots (if using), mixing well. Serve immediately.

There is a whole lot more to tomatoes in sauces than simply for pasta (but for that too, of course). There are raw tomato sauces for spooning over toast or serving with grilled fish; there are the sauces made with an extra-deep burst of tomato that can only happen when you use good tomato purée; there is a nutmeg and mascarpone sauce – the warm nuttiness of the spice segueing beautifully between the acidity of the tomatoes and the richness of the mascarpone; there's a sauce with saffron taking it's style notes from southern France; there's chilli, and butter, and also ghee; there are sauces using canned and sauces using peeled, fresh tomatoes – a little painstaking to do sometimes, but worth it for a result that is bright and glossy with tender, beautiful chunks of softened tomato flesh.

A tomato sauce can be many things, but one thing it must always be, is best quality. So, when you need fresh, use the ripest, sweetest and plumpest tomatoes you can. When you're using prepared, buy the best canned tomatoes or passata your budget can yield – I like San Marzano – it really will make all the difference. And, lastly, good tomato purée should taste just fine, as is, when squirted directly from the tube. It should taste of tomatoes left out in the sun, desiccating and drying, to the fullest and most rich-tasting version of themselves.

Sauces

Grated Raw Tomatoes for Garlic-rubbed Toast

400g (14oz) tomatoes, coarsely grated (shredded)

2 tablespoons good olive oil, plus more to serve

a pinch of dried oregano, or use finely chopped fresh oregano or marjoram leaves (optional)

4 slices of good-quality bread

1 garlic clove, halved

salt

Tomatoes on toast, sliced and looking lovely, are good, but grating them is a total game-changer. Not quite so startling to look at... nor, dare I say, to photograph, but grating tomatoes for the classic Spanish dish of Pan Catalan is what makes this the most sublime piece of toast you will ever, in your whole life, eat.

1. In a bowl, mix the grated tomato with the olive oil, and the herbs (if using), and a seasoning of salt.

2. Toast the slices of bread on both sides and rub the hot toast vigorously all over with the halved garlic clove.

3. Spoon the tomato mixture over the garlic toast and drizzle with a little extra olive oil. Serve.

Grated Raw Tomatoes with Ginger and Coriander

250–300g (9–10½oz) tomatoes,
   coarsely grated (shredded)
2cm (¾in) piece of fresh ginger
   (unpeeled is fine), grated (shredded)
1 tablespoon good olive oil

your chosen grilled (broiled) fish or meat
   (see introduction)
½ bunch of coriander (cilantro), leaves
   picked and roughly chopped
salt and freshly ground black pepper

As in the previous recipe, simply grating the tomatoes gives this sauce a dazzling purity in texture. Add grated fresh ginger to the mixture and you have a raw tomato sauce that has a warm, sweetly spiced pungency, well-seasoned and with a splash of olive oil for an extra fruity viscosity. This is a perfect match for grilled oily fish, such as mackerel or sardines; it would also be very good with roast chicken or pan-fried pork chops. So quick and easy to put together, some simply cooked green beans would be a fine companion.

1. In a mixing bowl, combine the tomatoes, ginger and olive oil, seasoning well with salt and plenty of pepper. The oil will not emulsify, that is the charm – a mottled, beautiful sauce.

2. Spoon the sauce on to 4 plates or 1 large platter, top with your chosen grilled fish or meat and scatter over the coriander.

Trapanese Sauce

40g (1½oz) skinned whole almonds
1–2 garlic cloves, chopped
½ small bunch of basil, leaves picked
350g (12oz) peeled tomatoes, deseeded
  and quartered
80ml (2½fl oz) good olive oil

salt and freshly ground black pepper
400g (14oz) pasta of choice
pecorino, finely grated (shredded),
  to serve (optional)

How did Genovese pesto become the powerhouse of no-cook pasta sauces? Very probably because the jarred version is so ubiquitous on the supermarket shelves. Trapanese pesto, however, if you did want to make your own rather than rely on Genovese-style shop-bought varieties, is an easy rival – good tomatoes, ripe and sweet, pulverized with skinned almonds, raw garlic, olive oil and basil, it is simple to make at home, pretty much in the time it takes for the pasta to boil. Some would say this is a no-cheese pasta dish, but I like to add a good shower of freshly grated pecorino to serve. Sheep's milk is more commonplace for cheese-making in Sicily than cow's, so pecorino makes more sense to me here than Parmesan.

1. Toast the almonds in a dry frying pan over a moderate heat, stirring often, for about 3 minutes, until fragrant and very lightly golden. Remove from the heat.

2. In a food processor, combine the toasted almonds, with the garlic and basil and pulse until well combined in a coarse rubble. Add the tomatoes and blitz briefly to break them down and loosen the pesto. Stir through the olive oil, then check the seasoning, adding salt and pepper to taste. Put to one side. (Alternatively, chop the lot on a large wooden chopping board, or use a pestle and mortar to grind, then add the mixture to a bowl and stir in the olive oil to combine.) Stored in a jar in the fridge under a layer of olive oil, the sauce will last well for up to 3 days.

3. To serve, cook the pasta according to the packet instructions, until al dente. Drain, reserving a little of the pasta cooking water. Return the pasta to the pan and stir though the Trapanese sauce, adding splash of the reserved cooking water to loosen. Sprinkle with a little pecorino to serve.

Raw Tomatoes and Garlic with Olive Oil

1kg (2lb 4oz) tomatoes, halved, seeds squeezed out
4 tablespoons good olive oil, plus more to serve
2 garlic cloves, crushed to a paste with a little salt

pinch of chilli flakes, to taste (optional)
500g (1lb 2oz) pasta of choice
salt and freshly ground black pepper
Parmesan, grated (shredded), to serve

Another no-cook pasta sauce, and this one could not be any easier. Chopped tomatoes, crushed garlic and olive oil, all seasoned with the knee-jerk trio of salt, pepper and chilli flakes. The only hint I will give to making this sauce the best version of itself, is do try to squeeze out some of the seeds when you prepare the tomatoes. It's not at all difficult – cut the tomato in half horizontally and give each half a good squeeze, as you would a lemon. The riper, the better for this one. And, if it's a hot day, or you have a warm spot in the kitchen, leave the prepared tomatoes in a bowl to warm ever so slightly, yielding to the seasoning, soaking in the olive oil for 30 minutes or more before you cook the pasta.

1. Finely chop the deseeded tomatoes and put them into a large bowl. Season well with salt and pepper, and add the olive oil, garlic and chilli flakes, if using. Mix well to combine, then set to one side somewhere warm for at least 30 minutes, ideally for an hour or two.

2. Cook the pasta in well-salted water according to the packet instructions, until al dente. Drain, reserving a little of the pasta cooking water. Return the pasta to the pan and stir through the tomato mixture, adding a little of the pasta cooking water to loosen, if needed.

3. Drizzle with a little more olive oil and sprinkle with the Parmesan to serve.

A Simple Cooked Tomato Sauce

4 tablespoons good olive oil
about 3 fat garlic cloves, unpeeled and
   slightly squashed, or peeled and finely
   chopped or sliced
1 x 400g (14oz) can of plum or cherry
   tomatoes
2 bay leaves
about 1 tablespoon finely chopped
   rosemary leaves

about 1 teaspoon dried oregano
big pinch of salt, plus more to taste
chilli flakes, to taste (optional)
about ½ small bunch of basil, oregano or
   marjoram
400g (14oz) pasta of choice
freshly ground black pepper
Parmesan, grated (shredded), to serve
   (optional)

This is the sauce I make time and again. It is the tomato sauce that can rescue any mismanaged mealtime, any 'I-have-no-idea-what-to-feed-anyone-this-evening' moments. Also, those scenarios with extra mouths to feed that no one quite warned you about. Canned tomatoes, two, three or even four garlic cloves (whole, skin removed for a gentler flavour, or peeled and sliced for a more assertive one), olive oil (a good amount), whatever herbs you have to hand, or not for that matter (dried oregano can be a winner here), and chilli flakes, for extra pep – the very essence of fast food. There are no hard-and-fast rules, so I'm giving you a very lose recipe – it's now yours to make your own.

1. Heat half the olive oil in a large frying pan or saucepan over a moderate heat (the wide surface area will cook the tomatoes faster). Add the garlic and cook for about 2 minutes until fragrant, but not browning. Add the tomatoes, herbs and salt, mashing the tomatoes down with the back of a wooden spoon in the pan. Add the chilli flakes, if using, add plenty of pepper.

2. Bring the tomatoes to a rapid simmer over a high heat, then turn down the heat and simmer for about 10–12 minutes to concentrate the flavours and thicken the sauce. Loosen with a little splash of water, mixing well to incorporate, if you want a looser texture.

3. Remove from the heat. Check the seasoning and adjust with salt, pepper and chilli flakes, if you like. Stir through the remainder of the olive oil, mixing to combine and to round off the flavours. Fish out the whole garlic before using.

4. Cook the pasta in well-salted water according to the packet instructions, until al dente. Drain, reserving a little of the pasta cooking water. Return the pasta to the pan and stir through sauce, adding a little of the pasta cooking water to loosen, if needed. Serve with grated (shredded) Parmesan, if you wish.

Puttanesca Sauce

4 tablespoons olive oil, plus more
  to serve
3–4 garlic cloves, very thinly sliced
1 teaspoon chilli flakes, or more to taste
80g (2¾oz) best-quality black olives,
  pitted and roughly chopped
2 tablespoons capers, rinsed if packed
  in salt, roughly chopped
1 tablespoon tomato purée
  (concentrated paste)

½ bunch of flat-leaf parsley, leaves
  picked and chopped
400g (14oz) tomatoes, chopped,
  or 400g (14oz) passata, or 1 x 400g
  (14oz) can of plum tomatoes, chopped
8 anchovies, rinsed if packed in salt,
  roughly chopped
400g (14oz) pasta of choice
salt and freshly ground black pepper
Parmesan, grated (shredded), to serve

A classic Neapolitan pasta sauce with, well, saucy, associations – so the story goes, this is a pasta sauce that prostitutes (or their taskmaster madams) would cook to sate themselves after work. Fiery, salty and rich, this deeply flavoured tomato sauce is a turbocharge for the tastebuds, a wake-up call for the overworked. Whatever the etymology – how it came to be, as a recipe documented or simply memorized by rote and favour – I think we can all agree that the combination of ingredients is a good one and the reason why it became such a staple of southern Italian cooking. Notoriety came later.

1. Heat the oil in a saucepan over a moderate heat. Add the garlic and fry for 2 minutes, until fragrant but not coloured, then add the chilli flakes, olives and capers. Add the tomato purée and half the parsley, stirring well to combine. Cook for about 30 seconds for the flavours to really ramp up.

2. Add the tomatoes and simmer vigorously for about 5 minutes, until the sauce is thick and rich-tasting. If you're using fresh tomatoes, a splash of water will help to get things going and encourage the sauce to cook, not stick too soon.

3. Check the seasoning, adding salt and pepper to taste, and more chilli flakes, if you like – it should be fairly hot from the chilli. Then, finally, add the anchovies. Remove the pan from the heat and stir to melt and soften the anchovies in the warm sauce.

4. Cook the pasta in well-salted boiling water according to the packet instructions until al dente. Drain, reserving a little of the pasta cooking water, then tip the pasta back into the pan. Stir through the pasta sauce, adding a little of the cooking water to loosen the sauce, if necessary.

5. Serve immediately with a slick more olive oil and some Parmesan and the remaining parsley scattered over.

Amatriciana Sauce

2 tablespoons olive oil
100g (3½oz) guanciale, pancetta or
  unsmoked streaky bacon, thinly sliced
  and chopped into 1cm (½in) pieces
½ teaspoon chilli flakes, or to taste

400g (14oz) tomatoes, roughly chopped,
  or 1 x 400g (14oz) can of plum
  tomatoes, roughly chopped
400g (14oz) pasta of choice
120g (4¼oz) pecorino or Parmesan,
  grated (shredded)
salt and freshly ground black pepper

Guanciale is cured pork jowl – it is a very different ingredient to pancetta or streaky bacon (both from the belly) and has a sweet, unctuous flavour. It's fairly easy to come by in bigger supermarkets and, of course, Italian grocery stores. This is a simple pasta dish that relies on the fat of the guanciale to render in the pan. There are a few tomatoes, not masses – this is a sauce of cooked salted pork and lots of freshly grated pecorino, flecked through and softened with tomato. And, although I've said how essential guanciale is to the recipe, if you happen to use pancetta or good unsalted streaky bacon, people won't come hammering on your front door demanding you throw the lot in the bin and begin again with guanciale. They really won't.

1. Heat the oil in a pan over a moderate heat. Add the guanciale or bacon and fry for about 4–5 minutes, until crisp and golden and the fat has rendered into the pan. Add the chilli flakes and stir to combine.

2. Add the tomatoes and cook for about 5–8 minutes, stirring often enough for the tomatoes to break down and to create a light sauce. Check the seasoning, remembering the guanciale is salty, and add salt and pepper accordingly.

3. Cook the pasta in well-salted boiling water according to the packet instructions until al dente. Drain, reserving a little of the pasta cooking water, then tip the pasta back into the pan. Stir through the tomatoes and three-quarters of the grated pecorino or Parmesan, adding a little of the pasta cooking water to loosen the sauce and amalgamate the cheese into it.

4. Serve with the remaining cheese at the table for people to help themselves.

Tomato, Sausage, Nutmeg and Mascarpone Sauce

2 tablespoons olive oil
1 small onion, finely chopped
6 sausages, meat squeezed from
   the casings
2 garlic cloves, finely chopped
½ teaspoon chilli flakes, or to taste
   (optional)

1 x 400g (14oz) can of plum tomatoes,
   drained and chopped
400g (14oz) pasta of choice, gnocchi
   or polenta
50g (1¾oz) mascarpone
¼ nutmeg, grated (shredded)
salt and freshly ground black pepper
Parmesan, grated (shredded), to serve

Now this really is a tomato sauce and a half. Use the best-quality canned tomatoes your budget can buy, and cook them down, down, down along with some sausage meat that has been squeezed from its casings (a dreamy task?), diced onions and garlic, and then showered with a beguiling quantity of freshly grated nutmeg – so much nutmeg, in fact, that you question yourself, and then carry on, knowing exactly why. Nutmeg is a favourite spice – warming with sweet notes. In this recipe it rounds off flavour, softening the acidity of the tomatoes and lending a sweetness to the saltiness of the sausage meat. Stirring through the mascarpone at the end further enriches the sauce, and turns it a shade of red that really should be listed in the Pantone library of reds.

1. Heat the oil in a pan over a moderate heat. Add the onion and fry for 10 minutes or so, until softened but not coloured. Add the sausage meat and cook until browning in places, then add the garlic and chilli flakes and fry for 1–2 minutes, until fragrant.

2. Add the tomatoes to the sausage mixture, seasoning well with salt and pepper, then lower the heat. Cook for about 10 minutes, until the sauce is thickened and rich.

3. While the sauce is cooking, cook your pasta or gnocchi in well-salted boiling water according to the packet instructions, until al dente in the case of the pasta or until the gnocchi float to the surface. Drain, reserving a little of the cooking water, then tip the pasta or gnocchi back into the pan. If you're using polenta, cook it according to the packet instructions – you can serve it like this, or set and fried in pieces.

4. Stir the mascarpone through the sausage and tomato mixture and add the nutmeg, mixing well to combine. Check the seasoning, adding salt and pepper to taste.

5. Serve with the pasta, gnocchi or polenta, sprinkled with plenty of Parmesan.

SAUCES

Patatas Bravas

500g (1lb 2oz) floury baking potatoes
120ml (4fl oz) olive or sunflower oil
1 onion, finely diced
2–4 garlic cloves, finely chopped,
 to taste
½–2 teaspoons chilli flakes or cayenne
 pepper, to taste
2 teaspoons smoked paprika, plus a bit
 more to serve

½ tablespoon red wine vinegar or
 sherry vinegar
1 x 400g (14oz) can of plum tomatoes,
 chopped
salt and freshly ground black pepper
100g (3½oz) aïoli (see pages 46 or
 156 for homemade), to serve

So called 'brave potatoes' for the spicy, smoky sauce that accompanies them. So, yes, I would urge you to be bold with the chilli, garlic and paprika. Which way will you choose to serve this classic Spanish tapas dish: potatoes on top of sauce or sauce on top of potatoes? As with all celebrated international recipes, there are many, many interpretations. Chefs up and down the country in Spain and everywhere else beyond will tell you in no uncertain terms, it's their road or the high road. Furthermore, I have it from a good, reliable source that a Spaniard would always blend the bravas sauce, never leave it chunky – but I'll leave you to experiment. I'm roasting the potatoes, because it's easier, but you could, of course, fry them.

1. Boil the potatoes whole with their skin on in well-salted water, until tender. Drain them, leave them to cool, and then peel them, discarding the skins. Cut them into 2.5cm (1in) cubes.

2. Preheat the oven to 220°C/200°C fan/425°F/Gas 7 and line a baking sheet with baking paper.

3. Douse the potato cubes in half the oil and a good sprinkling of salt and pepper. Roast them for about 20–25 minutes in the hot oven, giving them a shuffle midway through if you like, until well-coloured and turning crisp at the edges. Remove from the oven and put to one side.

4. Meanwhile, heat the remaining oil in a saucepan over a moderate heat. Add the onion and fry for about 10 minutes, until soft and translucent. Add the garlic and cook for 2 minutes more. Add the chilli flakes or cayenne pepper and the smoked paprika and cook for 30 seconds more. Add the vinegar and cook until it evaporates.

5. Add the tomatoes, season well with salt and pepper, then reduce the heat to moderate-low and simmer for about 15–20 minutes, until thick and rich. Check the seasoning, adjusting with more of anything, as necessary. Remove from the heat, but keep warm.

6. To serve, pile the lot on to a large serving plate, either sauce then potatoes or potatoes then sauce, dolloping the top with aïoli and dusting with a little extra paprika.

Zaalouk

1 large aubergine (eggplant)
3 tablespoons olive oil, plus more
   to serve
1 onion, finely diced
2 garlic cloves, finely chopped
400g (14oz) tomatoes, roughly chopped,
   or use 1 x 400g (14oz) can of plum
   tomatoes, roughly chopped
1 tablespoon tomato purée
   (concentrated paste)

1 teaspoon ground cumin
a big pinch of dried chilli flakes, plus
   more to taste
1 teaspoon unsmoked paprika (sweet or
   hot is fine)
salt and freshly ground black pepper
small bunch of coriander (cilantro),
   leaves picked and roughly chopped,
   to serve

*Pairing tomato with its best friend aubergine, this is a tried-and-tested combination,
and a duo that crops up in the many different countries that grow tomatoes and
aubergines. Zaalouk itself is a Moroccan dish, although it's popular throughout
North Africa. Serve with flat breads to scoop. As a side dish it would work beautifully
alongside some fried fish, lamb or chicken, but I could quite honestly eat it just as it is
– warm with a slick of good olive oil to serve.*

1. Set the grill (broiler) to high, or set the aubergine directly over a gas flame or hot
coals (I have a brilliant piece of Turkish cooking kit that sits over the burner, which
you then place the aubergine on to burn). Cook the aubergine until the skin is fully
blackened and the flesh is completely soft and collapsed. This takes time – about
15 minutes, or less or considerably more depending on the size of the aubergine.
Remove the aubergine from the heat and leave until cool enough to peel. Discard
the skin.

2. Heat the olive oil in a pan over a moderate heat. Add the onion and cook for about
10 minutes, until softened but not coloured. Add the garlic and cook for 1–2 minutes
more, until fragrant, then add the tomatoes, tomato purée and the spices and season
well with salt and freshly ground black pepper. Reduce the heat to moderate–low, put
a lid on the pan, and cook, covered, for about 10–15 minutes, until rich and thick.

3. On a board, roughly chop the cooled aubergine and stir it into the tomato sauce.
Cook gently for about 3 minutes, to fully heat through, the aubergine turning the
sauce thick and creamy. Check the seasoning, adding more salt and pepper, if
necessary, along with chilli flakes, to taste. Remove from the heat.

4. Spoon the tomatoes and aubergine out on to a plate and top with the coriander and
a slick more olive oil, to serve.

SAUCES

SERVES 4 AS
A SIDE DISH
OR LIGHT
APPETIZER,
WITH FLAT
BREADS

Tomatoes Cooked and Served with Mint, Chilli and Pine Nuts

1kg (2lb 4oz) tomatoes, ideally peeled (see page 37)
80ml (2½fl oz) olive oil or melted ghee
6 garlic cloves, thinly sliced
½–1 not-too-hot green chilli, finely chopped, to taste
½ teaspoon dried mint

2 tablespoons pine nuts (or use flaked almonds or walnut pieces)
a small bunch of mint, leaves picked and roughly chopped
salt and freshly ground black pepper
flat breads or pitas, warmed, to serve

Ideally, you'll peel the tomatoes for this recipe. Some kind of magic happens when you first fry garlic in olive oil, then add peeled, roughly chopped tomatoes, leaving them to stew just long enough to soften, turning an extraordinary, melt-in-the-mouth texture. Honestly, when testing this dish, it became one of my favourites in the book. It is sensational. Serve it with warm flat breads, good and plump to heat on a grill or barbecue, or in the oven, and serve as part of a multi-course meal, or to accompany grilled fish or meat or other vegetables. If you can't be bothered to peel the tomatoes, preferring to hurl them in skin on and chopped into the garlic and olive oil, this recipe will work out just fine, you just won't get the tenderness that comes from a tomato cooked without its skin. Nonetheless, the world will still turn, and this will still be utterly delicious. Use almonds or walnuts if pine nuts are exorbitant.

1. Cut the peeled tomatoes into slices of about 1cm (½in).

2. Heat half the olive oil or the ghee in a pan over a moderate heat. Add half the garlic and cook for 2 minutes, until fragrant. Add the tomatoes and chilli and season well to taste with salt and pepper.

3. Reduce the heat and simmer the sauce for 12–15 minutes, until thickened. Add the dried mint, stirring to combine, then remove from the heat.

4. Heat the remaining oil in a small pan over a moderate–high heat. Add the remaining garlic and cook until it just begins to turn lightly golden (about 3 minutes), then add the pine nuts (or almonds or walnuts) and cook for 30 or so seconds, until lightly golden and the garlic is by now golden brown. Remove from the heat.

5. Spread the cooked tomato out over a large plate or serving platter. Add the garlic and pine nuts and their flavoured cooking oil and, finally, the mint. Serve either warm or at room temperature with warmed flat breads or pitas.

Sweet Cinnamon Tomato Sauce

3 tablespoons olive oil or melted ghee

1 onion, finely diced

3 garlic cloves, finely chopped

2 bay leaves, scrunched a little

1 cinnamon stick or ½ teaspoon ground cinnamon

1 teaspoon ground coriander

½ teaspoon ground allspice (optional)

1 x 400g (14oz) can of plum tomatoes

chilli flakes, to taste (optional)

salt and freshly ground black pepper

This sauce is such a useful preparation. It's so versatile it will happily match our family-favourite rice dish of koshari – long grain or basmati rice cooked in stock with small pasta and also lentils. This cinnamon-scented tomato sauce (do use a whole cinnamon stick, one that has plenty of pep) is also a terrific match to serve alongside roast or fried chicken, or grilled lamb. Although you could opt for fresh tomatoes, I've used canned for this recipe, as I think it needs them. Seasoned yogurt is a good match to round off flavours. In contrast, to really boost flavour, butter, cooked until foaming and golden with nuts or seeds, adds all kinds of outrageousness.

1. Heat 2 tablespoons of the oil in a pan over a moderate heat. Add the onion and cook for about 10 minutes, until softened but not coloured. Add the garlic, bay leaves, cinnamon, ground coriander and allspice, if using, and cook for another 1–2 minutes, until fragrant.

2. Add the tomatoes and 100ml (3½fl oz) of water and season well with salt and pepper. Add the chilli flakes, if using. Bring the tomatoes to a simmer, then turn down the heat to low and cook for about 25–30 minutes, stirring from time to time.

3. Remove the pan from the heat and add the remaining olive oil, stirring to combine. Remove the cinnamon stick and bay leaves and serve warm.

Cherry Tomatoes Cooked
with Saffron and White Wine

SERVES 4

2 tablespoons olive oil, plus more
   to serve
2 large shallots, finely diced
1 garlic clove, finely sliced
1 large glass of dry white wine
   (about 175ml/5½fl oz)
1 bay leaf, scrunched a little
20 cherry tomatoes, quartered
   (or use 400g/14oz regular tomatoes,
   diced small)

½ teaspoon fennel seeds, crushed a little
200ml (7fl oz) fish stock or water
a big pinch of saffron threads
fish fillets of choice, or prawns (shrimp),
   for poaching
salt and freshly ground black pepper
½ small bunch of chives, finely chopped,
   to serve
¼ small bunch of flat-leaf parsley, finely
   chopped, to serve

This deceptively simple sauce is great to use as a poaching liquid for firm, fresh, white fish fillets or perhaps some prawns. The flavours speak to me of southern France, right down at the bottom of the country, where the sun shines hard and the heat of the day is long. This is an elegant sauce, one I might choose to serve alongside some couscous or boiled new potatoes. If you opt for potatoes, and you wanted to add an extra accompaniment, then the roasted tomato aïoli on page 42 would be a fine match. By all means add vegetables to the mixture if you like. Boil them briefly first in well-salted water until just cooked, then drain them and finish them off in the sauce, perhaps adjusting the liquid (wine or water) to accommodate. Green beans, fennel or celery would be especially good.

1. Heat the oil in a pan over a moderate heat. Add the shallots and cook for about 5 minutes until softened, but not coloured. Add the garlic and cook for 2 minutes, until fragrant.

2. Add the wine, turn up the heat and simmer fast for about 5 minutes to reduce the contents of the pan by about half.

3. Add the bay leaf, tomatoes, fennel seeds and stock or water, increase the heat to high and bring the contents of the pan up to a boil, then boil for 1 minute.

4. Add the saffron, along with some salt and pepper to taste, then simmer over a moderate heat for 5 minutes.

5. It is at this point that you can poach your fish or prawns – simply simmer them in the sauce over a moderate heat for 2–4 minutes, depending on the thickness of your fillets or size of your prawns. Remove from the heat once the fish or prawns are opaque and cooked through, then finish with the finely chopped herbs and a slick more olive oil to serve.

Deep-frying things seems to make people panic. Fair enough – boiling oil is hot and also volcanically dangerous, but as cookery practices go, so absolutely worth the effort. I'm here to encourage. If you don't have a deep-fat fryer, and many don't (myself included), use a high-sided saucepan, never filling the pan up with oil more than a third full. Do yourself a favour and buy a good digital thermometer to ensure the oil is at the correct temperature to deep-fry – too cold and anything you drop in will soak up the oil, turning flaccid and unappealing before the exterior is crisp and cooked; too hot and whatever you drop in will colour too quickly, leaving the interior undercooked, often inedible. The sweet spot for deep-frying is 170–180°C (325–350°F), turning all that you deep fry into something extremely delicious. Shallow-frying prompts less hesitancy in people, so I've included both methods in this chapter.

And one last thing to mention is that tomatoes do like to be fried. I'm not here to vouch for any so-called healthy eating practices – delicious ones are my chief focus. The contrast between the fruity, sweet acidity of a tomato and the oil that they come into contact with when frying really does something quite sublime for our tastebuds.

Fried & Grilled

Roasted Tomato Falafels with Tomato Yogurt, Pickles, Chopped Salad and Flat Breads

500g (1lb 2oz) tomatoes, halved, or use cherry tomatoes
2 tablespoons olive oil
2–3 garlic cloves, chopped
350g (12oz) dried chickpeas, soaked overnight in cold water, then drained
2 shallots, finely chopped
50g (1¾oz) smoked sundried tomatoes, drained and chopped, or use 2 tablespoons tomato purée (concentrated paste)
2 teaspoons ground coriander
2 teaspoons ground cumin
1 teaspoon unsmoked sweet paprika
1 teaspoon salt, plus more to season
neutral oil (such as sunflower or vegetable), for deep-frying
freshly ground black pepper

To serve
100g (3½oz) natural (plain) yogurt
tomatoes, cucumbers and spring onions (scallions), chopped into uniform dice and seasoned with a big pinch of salt and a squeeze of lemon
flat breads, warmed
1 heaped tablespoon tahini, mixed with a splash of warm water to the consistency of double (heavy) cream
hot sauce of choice (see page 25 to make your own)
Middle Eastern pickles (chilli, carrot, turnip and so on)
A small bunch of flat-leaf parsley, mint or coriander (cilantro), leaves picked and roughly chopped

Roasted tomatoes do something insane to the falafel mixture in this recipe, giving the falafel an extra-moist interior as well as a gorgeous, red-tinged crust. I've given a recipe for falafels in a previous book, but those were bright green and made with fava beans. This version is with chickpeas and brick-red in colour. Using half the roasted tomatoes in the falafel mixture and the other half in the seasoned yogurt really ramps up the profile of the tomato. Add a chopped salad, with yet more tomatoes, and this could be considered peak tomato. Original recipe published by The Tomato Stall (@iowtomatoes) and reprinted here with their kind permission.

1. Preheat the oven to 180°C/160°C fan/350°F/Gas 4.

2. Put the tomatoes, cut side up, in a roasting pan and drizzle with the olive oil. Sprinkle with a good seasoning of salt and roast for 15–25 minutes, until very soft and starting to caramelize a little. Remove from the oven and set aside to cool. Remove the roasted tomatoes from the pan, reserving any liquid left in the pan to add to the yogurt.

3. Using a food processor, blend the roasted tomatoes with the garlic until smooth. Set aside 100g (3½oz) of this mixture in a bowl, leaving the remainder in the food processor.

4. Add the chickpeas to the food processor, along with the shallots, sundried tomatoes or purée, the spices and salt and blend until you have a coarse paste. Chill the mixture in the fridge for at least 30 minutes.

continued overleaf

5. Heat a 5cm (2in) depth of oil in a saucepan over a moderate–high heat and fry off a teaspoon of the mixture to check the seasoning. Taste and adjust with more salt and pepper, if necessary.

6. Preheat the oven to 160°C/140°C fan/315°F/Gas 2–3.

7. Mix the reserved blended tomatoes and any tomato roasting juices with the yogurt for serving and season really well with salt. Transfer to a serving bowl and put to one side.

8. Test the oil temperature – you need it at 180°C/350°F on a digital thermometer (alternatively drop a thin slice of ginger or cube of bread into the oil – if it floats and sizzles, turning golden and crisp within 60 seconds, the oil is at a good temperature to deep-fry).

9. The mixture is quite wet and the oil is very hot, so do be careful from here. Using two spoons (one to shape and one to scrape the mixture off), drop spoonfuls of the batter into the hot oil – it should bubble and fry, quickly turning crisp and golden brown in about 2 minutes. Flip the falafels over to fry on the other side for 1½–2 minutes more. Work in small batches, 3 or 4 falafels at a time, removing the cooked falafels with a slotted spoon and setting them aside to keep warm in the oven while you make the next batch, until you've used up all the mixture.

10. To serve, pile some chopped tomato salad on to the flat breads, add some falafel, then the tomato-seasoned yogurt, a slick of tahini, hot sauce (if using), and some pickles and herbs.

Deep-fried Camembert Beignets with Tomatoes

50g (1¾oz) unsalted butter
1 teaspoon caster (superfine) sugar
75g (2½oz) plain (all-purpose) flour, sifted
2 eggs, beaten
neutral oil (such as sunflower or vegetable oil), for deep-frying

50g (1¾oz) camembert (rind on is fine), cut into 5-10mm (¼-½in) cubes
salt and freshly ground black pepper
tomato sauce (see page 93), to serve
Parmesan, grated (shredded), to serve

This is a favourite recipe in the book for me. Think of the beignet as a little doughnut stuffed with camembert cheese, which melts obediently once deep-fried. At the same time, the skin of the choux pastry turns crisp and golden, a perfect mouthful. Served on a pool of tomato sauce, then showered with plenty of freshly grated Parmesan, these really are all kinds of incredible.

1. Put the butter and sugar in a saucepan with 150ml (5fl oz) of water and place it over a high heat. As soon as the mixture begins to boil, vigorously mix in the flour, beating well until you have a smooth dough that pulls away from the sides of the pan in a shiny, cohesive mass.

2. Remove from the heat and allow to cool for about 3–5 minutes, beating the dough vigorously at least a couple of times.

3. Add the eggs one at a time, beating them in hard and continuously with a wooden spoon, until completely combined. Season with salt and pepper and put to one side.

4. Fill a deep, heavy-based saucepan one-third full of neutral oil and place it over a moderate–high heat. Add a small piece of batter to test the heat - it should sizzle at the surface, turning golden brown within 30 seconds. If you have a digital thermometer, 170°C/325°F is a good frying temperature.

5. Using 2 teaspoons, shape spoonfuls of the dough roughly to the size of a ping-pong ball, then push a piece of camembert into the middle, moulding the cheese within the dough. This is a messy task – don't fret, rough-hewn is good. Just make sure the cheese is sealed within the dough.

6. One at a time, carefully drop the balls of filled choux dough into the pan of hot oil, taking care not to overcrowd it - say batches of 3 or 4 at a time. Fry each batch for about 4–5 minutes, until the balls have all risen to the surface and are nicely golden brown and crisp. Remove with a slotted spoon and drain them on a plate lined with kitchen paper. Keep going until you've fried all the balls.

7. Serve the beignets hot on a pool of warm tomato sauce and sprinkled with plenty of Parmesan.

Fried Breakfast Tomatoes with Sausages and Bacon on Tomato Eggy Bread

SERVES 4

4 eggs

1 heaped teaspoon tomato purée (concentrated paste)

30g (1oz) smoked cheese (cheddar or similar), grated (shredded)

vegetable or sunflower oil, for frying

4 sausages

8 smoked or unsmoked, streaky or back bacon rashers (slices)

400g (14oz) tomatoes (4 small bunches on the vine is perfect, or use 4 larger tomatoes, halved)

4 thick (3cm/1½in) slices of slightly stale, good-quality white bread

a knob of butter

salt and freshly ground black pepper

breakfast sauce of choice (brown, ketchup or hot), to serve

I love tomato purée for its unbeatably intense tomato flavour (do buy best-quality). Here it's beaten with the eggs for tomato eggy bread, served alongside some fried halved tomatoes and also sausages, for those who wish. For breakfast, or brunch, or, indeed, lunch or dinner. Gives the phrase 'fry up' a whole new perspective.

1. Beat the eggs in a bowl along with the tomato purée and the grated cheese. Season well with salt and pepper and put to one side.

2. Heat a splash of oil in a frying pan over a moderate heat. Add the sausages and cook for about 5–8 minutes (depending on the size of the sausage), until browned and cooked through. Add the bacon and fry until cooked to your liking. Remove both from the pan and keep warm. Keep any fat behind in the pan.

3. Add a splash more oil to the pan, season the tomatoes well with salt and pepper and add them, cut-side up if using halved tomatoes, to the pan over a moderate heat. Put a lid on the pan, lower the heat a fraction and cook for 8–10 minutes, until the tomatoes are softened and cooked through. Uncover and cook until all the moisture has evaporated and the tomatoes are nicely browned underneath.

4. While the tomatoes are cooking, heat a splash of oil in a large frying pan over a moderate heat. Dip the bread in the eggy mixture for about 20 seconds, flipping each slice over to ensure both sides are evenly soaked and soft.

5. With the pan hot, fry the eggy bread for 2 minutes on each side, until golden (work in batches if you need to). Add the butter to the pan towards the end of the frying time, spooning the foaming butter over the fried bread.

6. Serve the cooked eggy bread immediately alongside the sausages, bacon and tomatoes, with sauce on the side for helping yourselves.

FRIED & GRILLED

Frying Pan Pizza with Tomato, Oregano and Chilli Flakes

For the dough

500g (1lb 2oz) '00' flour, or use plain (all-purpose) flour, plus more to roll

325ml (11fl oz) warm water

1½ teaspoons or 7g (⅙oz) fast-action dried yeast

1 teaspoon salt

For the topping

olive oil, for frying

1 x 400g (14oz) can of plum tomatoes, blended

1 tablespoon dried oregano (or use chopped fresh leaves, if you like)

4 garlic cloves, peeled and kept whole but bashed a little

salt and freshly ground black pepper

Parmesan, grated (shredded), to serve (optional)

Honestly a brilliant method to cook pizza. You do get a different kind of crust when you fry a pizza compared with baking one – different but just as good. It puffs in the pan, the dough blistering in patches and turning chewy from the oil. I've opted not to include any mozzarella, finding that if you do, you then need to put the grill (broiler) or oven on to melt the cheese enough. I want you to just use a frying pan, so this is pizza in the style of a marinara, or pizza rossa, a traditional Neapolitan pizza offering using just tomato sauce, olive oil, garlic and oregano. For the cheese hit, I've then opted to simply scatter the surface of the cooked pizza with freshly grated Parmesan, but you can opt to remain cheeseless.

1. Mix the flour, water and yeast together in a bowl to form a wet dough, then add the salt and put the dough to one side for 5 minutes.

2. Process the dough in a stand mixer fitted with a dough hook, kneading for 3–5 minutes, until smooth and cohesive (or do this by hand, if you like). Put to one side somewhere warm to rise for 1–2 hours, until not quite doubled in size.

3. Meanwhile, heat a splash of oil in a small saucepan over a moderate heat. Add the tomatoes, oregano and garlic, season well with salt and pepper and cook for about 10 minutes to thicken slightly and for the flavours to meld. Remove the garlic cloves from the tomato sauce, take the pan off the heat and put it to one side. This should be enough sauce for 4 pizzas.

4. Divide the risen dough equally into 4 balls and, on a lightly floured surface, roll or pull the dough into shape – about a 20cm (8in) disk, or to fit the size of your frying pan. Allow for each pizza to have a slightly bigger lip around the edge.

continued overleaf

5. Get the frying pan hot over a high heat. Add a big splash of olive oil (enough to cover the base of the frying pan) and, using tongs, gently lay one of the pizza disks into the pan, lowering it away from you, so you don't splash yourself with any of the hot oil.

6. Use the kitchen tongs to press the centre of the dough down as it bubbles up and away from the pan. Cook for about 1–1½ minutes on the first side, until golden brown in patches and bubbly on the surface. Use the tongs to carefully flip the dough over and cook the other side for another 1–2 minutes, until golden and bubbly in places.

7. Immediately slather the pizza with some of the tomato sauce, remove from the heat and add a slick more olive oil and a sprinkling of Parmesan, if you like, to serve. Repeat for the remaining disks of dough and the remaining topping sauce, serving the pizzas hot as they come out of the pan.

Fried Potato Cakes with Tomato and Parmesan

1.2kg (2lb 12oz) floury baking potatoes
150g (5½oz) tomatoes
2 egg yolks
30g (1oz) butter, melted
50g (1¾oz) plain (all-purpose) or
  '00' flour
olive oil, for frying, plus extra to serve

salt and freshly ground black pepper
radicchio or treviso, to serve (optional)
small bunch of herbs (chives, basil,
  dill, oregano, marjoram and flat-leaf
  parsley, say), chopped, to serve
Parmesan, shaved, to serve

You will need floury potatoes for this recipe to turn into meltingly soft potato cakes topped with peeled, thinly sliced tomatoes, a good amount of herbs and some Parmesan. It's the contrast between crisp, soft fried potato and the raw peeled tomato on top that I find so appealing.

1. Preheat the oven to 180°C/160°C fan/350°F/Gas 4.

2. Pierce the potatoes several times with the tip of a sharp knife and bake on a baking sheet for 45 minutes–1 hour, or until fluffy and tender.

3. While the potatoes are baking, bring a large pan of water to a boil. Slash the skin of each tomato with a sharp knife and plunge the tomatoes into the boiling water for 10 seconds. Remove with a slotted spoon, then place the tomatoes under cold running water or into a bowl of iced water for 30 seconds to arrest any further cooking. Remove from the cold water and then the skins should slip off easily. Thinly slice the peeled tomatoes, draining them on a plate, and put to one side.

4. When the potatoes are cooked through, cut them in half and scoop the flesh into a bowl. Use a ricer or potato masher and process until smooth. Season well with salt and pepper and, while the potato is still warm, beat in the egg yolks and butter. Scatter the flour over the mixture and mix briefly to combine.

5. Divide the mixture into 4 equal portions and shape each into a disk.

6. Heat a frying pan over a moderate heat and add a splash of oil. Carefully place the potato cakes in the hot oil and fry for 3–4 minutes, until golden brown on the underside. You may need to work in batches – don't overcrowd the pan. Flip the potato cakes over and fry until golden brown on the other side and piping hot throughout.

7. Arrange the potato cakes on a serving plate and top with a good amount of the thinly sliced tomatoes. Radicchio or treviso or any bitter leaf is nice here, the herbs and Parmesan complement the tomatoes too. Add a splash of good olive oil to serve.

Tomatoes Fried Hard with Chilli and Pork

5-10 dried bird's eye chillies, depending on how hot you can take it
boiling water, from a kettle
½ teaspoon salt, plus more to season
2 shallots, roughly chopped
1 lemongrass stalk, roughly chopped
4 garlic cloves, roughly chopped
2 tablespoons Thai fish sauce
1 heaped teaspoon fermented Thai soybean paste or miso
1 tablespoon light soy sauce
400g (14oz) cherry tomatoes, halved
vegetable oil, for frying

200g (7oz) minced (ground) pork
½ bunch of spring onions (scallions), thinly sliced

To serve
1 cucumber, sliced into half moons
½ small white cabbage or gem lettuce, cut into wedges
a handful of flat green beans, raw and trimmed
air-dried pork skin or pork scratchings
a small bunch of Thai basil or coriander (cilantro), leaves picked

This is inspired by a northern Thai dish called nam prik ong and one I thoroughly enjoyed eating (although it did annihilate my tastebuds) at the tail end of a long and brilliant trip overland from Beijing to Bangkok. For the dish to be considered a success, the application of chilli must be fierce, so don't stint, be bold. Traditionally served as a dip alongside an assortment of crunchy vegetables, it may also be served with air-dried crackly pork skin. Some Asian grocery stores will sell this, although you could, at a push, instead use pub-style pork scratchings. The tomatoes here bring sweet acidity and balance to the seasoning of the dish.

1. In a dry frying pan or wok over a moderate heat, toast the whole dried chillies for about 3 minutes, until smoking hot and fragrant – take care not to burn them. Put the chillies in a small bowl and cover with boiling water. Leave to rehydrate for 10 minutes or so. Once the chillies are soft, remove them from the water and roughly chop them.

2. Put the salt and rehydrated, chopped chillies in a mortar or food processor and pound or process until somewhat smooth. Then, add the shallots, lemongrass and half the garlic, pounding or processing to a paste. Next, add the fish sauce, soybean paste or miso, soy sauce and tomatoes, pounding or processing until most of the tomatoes are broken down, with a few still-recognizable shapes.

3. Get the frying pan or wok smoking hot over a high heat. Add 2 tablespoons of oil and add the remaining garlic, sautéing until golden. Add the tomato paste, stirring to combine. Cook this for 2 minutes to thicken slightly, then add the pork. Cook over a high heat, stirring continuously, for about 4–5 minutes, until the pork is piping hot and cooked through. Check the seasoning, adding a pinch of salt or more soy or fish sauce, to taste. Remove from the heat and top with the spring onions.

4. Serve the warm pork and tomato mixture with raw vegetables and pork skin for dipping, adding herb leaves to each mouthful.

Stir-fried Tomato Eggs

4 eggs

3 tablespoons neutral oil (such as sunflower or vegetable)

400g (14oz) tomatoes, cut into wedges, cored and deseeded

½ bunch of spring onions (scallions) or Chinese chives, trimmed and cut into 3cm (1¼in) pieces

a big pinch of caster (superfine) sugar

salt and freshly ground black pepper

This is a Chinese method for stir-frying eggs. As a 20-something-year-old chef, I had been asked to go and work in a restaurant in Chengdu to teach a young brigade of chefs how to make British-style savoury pies (one of my more obscure, and certainly most enjoyable cheffing jobs). My pastry-making and pie-crimping teaching done for the day, I happily anticipated the staff meals. With a keen eye, I'd watch as the Chinese chefs assembled lunch for the many, many employees who worked in the restaurant. These eggs took seconds to cook – so simple and with a bigger pinch of sugar than you might imagine. I loved them. They are so different from all the painstaking pies I was asked to produce – I know which one I'd rather eat now, just as I did back then. We ate this for lunch with steamed rice and Chinese pickles.

1. Crack the eggs into a bowl and season well with salt and pepper. Whisk vigorously for a few minutes until the mixture becomes pale and frothy.

2. Heat the oil in a wok or deep frying pan over a high heat until very hot – the oil should be shimmering. Then, very carefully stir in the egg. Once it's all in, don't mix it for about 10 seconds, then immediately turn off the heat and use a spatula to divide the egg into smaller pieces. Transfer the pieces to a plate and leave the hot oil behind in the wok or pan.

3. Reheat the oil until very hot once again, then add the tomatoes, stir-frying for 2–3 minutes, until softened, juicy and collapsed. Add the spring onions, then return the cooked egg to the pan, tossing in the pinch of sugar, and perhaps some extra salt and pepper, to taste. Serve immediately.

Breadcrumbed Tomatoes Baked in Cream with Fried Chicken

2 large, skinless chicken breasts, cut horizontally to about 2cm (¾in) thick, or 4 boneless and skinless thighs
100ml (3½fl oz) double (heavy) cream
1 small garlic clove, finely chopped
3 thyme or rosemary sprigs, leaves picked and finely chopped
1 teaspoon Dijon mustard
5 tablespoons plain (all-purpose) flour

300g (10½oz) panko breadcrumbs (or any other dried breadcrumbs)
3 eggs
500g (1lb 2oz) tomatoes, thickly sliced
6 tablespoons olive oil
30g (1oz) Parmesan, grated (shredded)
30g (1oz) butter
salt and freshly ground black pepper
1 lemon, cut into wedges, to serve

If you are going to go to the trouble of flouring, egging and breadcrumbing an ingredient – or pane, *to use the French term – I feel that you might as well get your hands really dirty and process a whole lot. In this case that means the tomatoes and the chicken, then going one step further and drenching the tomatoes in cream and mustard and baking them as a gratin until bubbling and blistering to serve alongside the fried chicken. A green salad, dressed simply, or some boiled green beans, might be a good serving suggestion.*

1. Using a meat mallet or rolling pin, flatten the chicken breasts out between 2 sheets of baking paper until they are an even 5mm (¼in) thick. Put to one side.

2. Preheat the oven to 200°C/180°C fan/400°F/Gas 6.

3. In a bowl or jug mix, together the cream, garlic, herbs and mustard and season well with salt and freshly ground black pepper. Put to one side.

4. Tip the flour into a wide, shallow bowl and the breadcrumbs into another. In a third bowl, beat the eggs with 2 tablespoons of water.

5. Season the tomatoes with salt and pepper, then dredge them in the flour, tapping off any excess. Dip them into the egg and then coat them in the breadcrumbs and put to one side.

6. Season the chicken pieces with salt and pepper, then dredge them in the flour, tapping off any excess. Dip the floured chicken pieces in the egg and then coat them with the breadcrumbs. Transfer the pieces to a plate and refrigerate until you're ready to cook.

7. Heat half the oil in a large frying pan over a high heat. Working in batches, fry the tomatoes for 1–2 minutes on each side, until golden all over. Slide the fried tomatoes out into a baking dish and pour over the cream mixture. Sprinkle with the Parmesan and bake the tomatoes for about 10–15 minutes, until golden and bubbling. Remove from the oven and keep warm.

continued overleaf

8. While the tomato gratin is baking, heat the remaining oil and half the butter in a large frying pan over a high heat. When the mixture begins to bubble and foam, add the coated chicken pieces and cook them over a high–moderate heat for about 3 minutes on each side, until crisp and golden and cooked through. Take care not to let the butter burn. If it starts to look like it might, add more to the pan, which should help prevent it turning completely. Remove the pan from the heat and drain the chicken pieces on kitchen paper.

9. Serve the chicken whole, or cut in half or into thick strips, with the tomato gratin alongside and lemon wedges for squeezing over.

Pan-fried Cherry Tomato and Caper Vinaigrette for Mackerel and Skordalia

SERVES 4

For the skordalia

250g (9oz) floury potatoes, washed but not peeled

3 garlic cloves, crushed to a fine paste with a pinch of salt

200ml (7fl oz) olive oil

finely grated zest and juice of 1 lemon

boiling water from a kettle, if needed

salt and freshly ground black pepper

For the rest

5 tablespoons good olive oil, plus more to serve

1 red onion, finely chopped

2 garlic cloves, finely chopped

400g (14oz) cherry tomatoes

2 tablespoons red wine vinegar

25g (1oz) capers, drained or soaked if salted; or 25g (1oz) green olives, pitted

½ small bunch of flat-leaf parsley, leaves picked and finely chopped

1 or 2 mackerel fillets per person (depending on size), pin boned

2 tablespoons plain (all-purpose) flour

a pinch or more of chilli flakes, to taste (optional)

1 lemon, cut into wedges, to serve

In this recipe the tomatoes form an almost-dressing that gets spooned over mackerel – and skordalia, a Greek dish of whipped potatoes with olive oil, lemon and lots of garlic. You can serve the skordalia warm or at room temperature, but never really piping hot. It's a perfect foil for the fish and tomatoes in this recipe.

1. First, make the skordalia. Boil the potatoes in their skins in plenty of well-salted water, until tender. Then, drain and while they're still hot (but manageable), peel them. The skins should come of pretty easily.

2. Push the potatoes through a sieve with a spoon, or use a mouli or a ricer, to form a smooth purée. Add the garlic, stirring to combine. Beat the olive oil and the juice and zest of the lemon into the potatoes, stirring to combine. You're looking for a fairly whippy, creamy consistency – add a splash of boiling water, if necessary, mixing well to combine. Check the seasoning, adding salt and pepper, to taste.

3. To make the dish, heat 2 tablespoons of the olive oil in a good, non-stick frying or cast-iron pan over a moderate-low heat. Add the onion and fry for about 10 minutes, until softened but not coloured. Add the garlic and cook for 2 minutes, until fragrant.

4. Add the cherry tomatoes, turn up the heat to moderate-high and fry for about 5 minutes, until the tomatoes begin to collapse and soften.

5. Stir in the vinegar and capers and cook for 1 minute for the flavours come together, then stir in the parsley and pour this dressing into a small bowl. Wipe out the pan.

6. Season the mackerel fillets with a little salt and pepper, then dust the skins with the flour.

continued overleaf

7. Add the remaining oil to the pan and turn up the heat to high. Carefully lay the mackerel fillets skin-side down into the hot oil and fry for 1 minute before turning the heat down to moderate and cooking for another 1½–3 minutes, depending on thickness. Carefully flip the fillets over and cook on the other side for 30 seconds or so, until the flesh is just opaque. Spoon over the tomato and caper dressing. Remove the pan from the heat.

8. To serve, divide the skordalia between the serving plates, then top with the mackerel fillets, making sure to scoop over plenty of the dressing. Sprinkle with chilli flakes, if you like, and serve with wedges of lemon for squeezing over.

Ribboned Crêpes Baked with Tomato Sauce and Mozzarella

4 eggs, beaten
85g (3oz) plain (all-purpose) flour
250ml (9fl oz) whole milk
½ teaspoon salt
butter, for greasing
1 recipe quantity of tomato sauce
  (see page 93), warmed

2 x 125g (4½oz) balls of mozzarella,
  drained and coarsely grated
  (shredded) or thinly sliced
80g (2¾oz) pecorino or Parmesan,
  grated (shredded)

A year or so ago, I spent some time out in Sicily at The Anna Tasca Lanza Cookery School. I found the school intoxicating, such was the devotion to food and local ingredients and the principles of good cookery practice. I was there in late autumn, so fresh tomatoes weren't really on the bill, but in the larder were jars and jars (too many to count) of homemade passata, processed at the tail end of the summer from the school's almighty tomato harvest. 'It must last us through to next summer – we must never run out, this would be a disaster,' said Fabrizia Lanza, owner of the school. I bought Fabrizia's book Coming Home to Sicily *and read it cover to cover on the flight home. This recipe jumped out at me as frugal, thoughtful and imaginative. I'm reproducing it here with her permission. I especially enjoy the thought of making the crêpes, then shredding them to serve as something entirely new and different, almost noodle-like.*

1. Tip the eggs into a medium bowl and whisk in the flour, a little at a time, until fully incorporated. Whisk in the milk and salt to form a smooth batter.

2. Grease a 23cm (9in) non-stick crêpe or omelette pan with butter and heat it over a medium heat. When the pan is hot, pour in enough batter to make a thickish crêpe, swirling to coat. Cook for about 1 minute, until the top sets, then flip the crêpe and cook it on the other side for about 30 seconds. As you cook the crêpes, transfer them to a plate and repeat the process until you have used up all the batter, making a stack.

3. Cut through the stack of crêpes to give you a mound of 1cm (½in) ribbons. Set the crêpe ribbons to one side.

4. Preheat the oven to 180°C/160°C fan/350°F/Gas 4 and grease a 23–30cm (9–12in) baking dish with butter.

5. Very gently mix two-thirds of the warm tomato sauce with the ribboned crêpes. Spread half the mixture out into an even layer in the prepared dish, then scatter over the mozzarella to cover. Top with the remaining crêpe ribbons and pour on the remaining sauce. Finally, sprinkle with the pecorino or Parmesan.

6. Bake the dish for about 20 minutes, until the sauce is bubbling and the topping is golden. Remove from the oven and let the dish stand for 10 minutes before serving.

Tomato and Saffron Arancini

about 1.2kg (2lb 12oz) leftover tomato and saffron risotto (see page 162), fridge-cold
10 small cherry-sized mozzarella balls, such as ciliegine or bocconcini
about 5 tablespoons plain (all-purpose) flour, for dusting

300g (10½oz) panko or other dried breadcrumbs
4 eggs, beaten
neutral oil (such as sunflower or vegetable), for deep-frying
Parmesan, grated (shredded), to serve
1 lemon, cut into wedges, to serve

There is a rule written somewhere in an enormously important cookery book that states when making risotto you must always make twice the amount so you can make arancini the following day. If you don't, you lack credibility both as a cook and as someone who cares deeply about the basic human right to eat arancini multiple times a year. If you eat enough of these, there is a hill, probably somewhere rural in Sicily, which you will need – if nothing else, to lie down on and take a nap. Original recipe published by The Tomato Stall (@iowtomatoes) and reprinted here with their kind permission.

1. Using wet hands, take a clementine-sized handful of the leftover risotto and compress it into a ball shape. Insert your thumb into the centre and place a piece of mozzarella into the space. Mould the rice around the mozzarella, creating a sealed ball. Repeat until you have 10 balls. Put to one side on a plate.

2. Tip the flour into a wide, shallow bowl, the breadcrumbs into another and the beaten egg into a third.

3. Gently roll each of the risotto balls first in the flour, then the egg and finally the breadcrumbs, compressing and compacting as much of the breadcrumb mixture as you can on to the surface of the risotto ball.

4. Preheat the oven to 180°C/160°C fan/350°F/Gas 4 and line a baking sheet with baking paper.

5. One-third fill a deep-sided saucepan with oil and heat it until it reads 180°C/350°F on a digital cooking thermometer (never fill the pan more than one-third full, as the oil will bubble up). Alternatively drop in a thin slice of ginger or a cube of bread and if it floats and sizzles to the top of the oil within 60 seconds, the oil is at a good temperature to deep-fry.

6. Working in batches, carefully deep-fry 2 or 3 arancini at a time (more will reduce the oil temperature too much) for about 3–5 minutes, until golden brown and very crisp. Remove each batch from the oil with a slotted spoon, place the arancini on the lined baking sheet and then into the oven to continue heating through while you fry the remainder. About 8 minutes in the oven should ensure the arancini are hot through and the mozzarella is beginning to melt.

7. Once all the arancini are ready, serve them sprinkled with Parmesan and with lemon wedges on the side for squeezing over.

Deep-fried Cauliflower with Tomato and Arbol Chilli Sauce

2 tablespoons olive oil
1 onion, finely chopped
3 garlic cloves, finely chopped
a big pinch of arbol chilli flakes
  (or regular flakes), plus more to taste
750g (1lb 10oz) tomatoes, roughly
  chopped
200ml (7fl oz) chicken or vegetable
  stock
1 cauliflower, cut into bitesize pieces
250g (9oz) green beans, cut into 2–3cm
  (¾–1¼in) pieces

neutral oil (such as sunflower or
  vegetable), for deep-frying
3 eggs
80g (2¾oz) plain (all-purpose) flour,
  seasoned with salt and pepper
salt and freshly ground black pepper

To serve
boiled white rice to serve 4
4–8 soft tortillas
hot sauce of choice (see page 25 to
  make your own)

The recipe is for chayotes capeadas en salsa jitomate, *which google translates as 'chayotes weathered in tomato sauce' and it is a brilliant and original recipe. I first spotted Cristina Martinez on Netflix via the* Chef's Table *series. I wrote to her and asked if she would be so kind as to give me an authentic Mexican recipe that makes use of tomatoes. She suggested cauliflower in lieu of chayotes, and she kindly corrected my trial run of the recipe that I sent through with photos of the dish for her to check, in which I served the fried cauliflower on top of the tomato sauce. Rather, she said, the tomato sauce must be more like a broth, to pour over the top of the cauliflower, which you then break up to eat in a taco. This recipe is completely delicious. Serve with rice and a soft tortilla, and extra-hot sauce of choice. Original recipe published by The Tomato Stall (@iowtomatoes) and reprinted here with their kind permission.*

1. Heat the olive oil in a pan over a moderate heat. Add the onion and fry for about 10 minutes, until softened but not coloured. Add the garlic and cook for 2 minutes, until fragrant. Add the chilli flakes and tomatoes, seasoning well to taste with salt and pepper.

2. Increase the heat to a simmer, then reduce the heat again to moderate and cook with a lid on for about 10 minutes, until the tomatoes have softened. Add the stock, bring the liquid back to a boil, reduce the heat to moderate and cook for 5 minutes. Remove from the heat and blend until smooth.

3. Bring a large pan of salted water to a boil. Tip in the cauliflower and boil for 4–5 minutes, until just tender, then remove with a slotted spoon and drain well. Leave to cool. Leave the pan on the heat.

4. Boil the green beans in the same water for 4–6 minutes, until completely tender, then drain and leave to one side.

continued overleaf

5. One-third fill a deep-sided saucepan with cooking oil and carefully heat it up until very hot – the temperature should read 180°C (350°F) on a digital cooking thermometer. If you don't have one, the oil is ready when you drop a piece of cauliflower into the pan and it sizzles and floats straight to the surface and turns golden within 30 seconds.

6. Whisk the eggs until they are very frothy, pale and creamy (ideally using an electric hand whisk). Tip the seasoned flour into a shallow bowl, and the beaten eggs into another.

7. Toss the drained, cold cauliflower in the seasoned flour, then coat each of the cauliflower pieces in the beaten eggs, carefully covering all the nooks and crannies. Work in batches, coating and then frying 2 or 3 pieces at a time, for about 2–3 minutes per batch, until pale golden and crisp, flipping the pieces over halfway through frying. As each batch is cooked, remove it from the oil and set it aside to drain on a large plate lined with kitchen paper while you fry the remainder.

8. While you're frying, add the blanched green beans to the sauce and heat them through, if necessary. Check the seasoning, adding more salt and chilli flakes, as needed.

9. Put all the fried cauliflower in a large serving dish and drench the lot with the tomato sauce. Serve with boiled rice, soft tortilla and hot sauce. Some fresh chilli and chopped coriander (cilantro) can be a nice addition, but are not detailed in Cristina's original recipe.

Scorched Tomatoes, Peppers and Aubergines with Sherry Vinegar and Anchovies

1kg (2lb 4oz) tomatoes
2 large red (bell) peppers
2 large aubergines (eggplants)
3 tablespoons olive oil, plus more
　to serve
2–3 garlic cloves, finely chopped
　or sliced

1 tablespoon sherry vinegar or red wine
　vinegar, or to taste
salt and freshly ground black pepper
8–10 best-quality anchovies in oil,
　drained, to serve (optional)

Cook this recipe when this trio of vegetables is in abundance – during high summer. Ideally you would blacken and scorch them over a barbecue or grill, scenting them with the wood smoke or charcoal as they soften – but, of course, feel free to use the grill (broiler) of your oven. I have a very nifty, and certainly not expensive piece of kit that sits on top of my gas burner – it's a wide, thin aluminium plate called a közmatik, a Turkish cooking utensil with vents that you use to obliterate your veg over a scorching heat, rendering the insides completely soft and the skin completely burned and collapsing in on itself. I'm serving the dish as a side, but for something more substantial, try it alongside some garlic-rubbed toast and/or fried eggs.

1. Heat the grill (broiler) to high, or use a barbecue at a moderate–high, but not flaming, heat.

2. Grill all the vegetables, turning them every now and then, until the skins are charred and the insides are collapsing and soft throughout. This can take anything from 5–20 minutes, depending on the vegetable – the aubergines will take the longest.

3. Remove the very, very soft vegetables from the heat. Leave them until cool enough to handle, then remove and discard the skins and remove the pepper seeds.

4. Roughly chop the flesh of everything and combine it in a serving bowl with the olive oil and the raw garlic. Season to taste with salt and pepper and the vinegar.

5. To serve, add a little more olive oil, if you like, and arrange the anchovy fillets on top. I like anchovies, so would use plenty (at least 8–10), but it's really up to you.

What strikes me about this chapter is the thoroughly international scope of it. Typically, braising is a combination-cooking technique, first searing an ingredient, then finishing the cook time in a stock, broth or sauce. It is the practice of cooking an ingredient in its own juices, which happens the world over. Tomatoes seem intrinsic to so much slow-cooked braising, thickening and flavouring the liquid as they do, along with every other ingredient in the pot. The juices go on to permeate the food, giving depth to the finished dish. Of course, there are exceptions to the searing, then adding process: the tagine (see page 146) is a case in point; as is the butter chicken (see page 140), where you have the option to first chargrill, then add the chicken to the sauce – or to not, it's up to you.

There's something else that brings a smile to my face in this chapter: the very red colour palette that all these dishes share. It's like a culinary pantone chart, from brick-red to beet-red to red-red, the tomatoes obliterated by time and heat, marking this chapter, perhaps, as one of the most tonally challenging to document when it comes to the photography. 'Look!' I said to photographer and friend Sam Folan. 'This chapter is all mostly very red and wet, sort of soupy-looking.' In retrospect, I think there must be some special kind of award that food writers and chefs should give to photographers to recognize the challenge they face when presented with an entire cookery book of very red-looking recipes. Whatever the award, Sam – you've definitely won it.

Braised & Stovetop

Butter Chicken

600g (1lb 5oz) skinless, boneless chicken thighs, diced into 3cm (1¼in) pieces

75g (2½oz) full-fat natural (plain) yogurt

juice of ½ lemon

3 tablespoons tandoori spice blend

60g (2oz) ghee or butter (or a neutral oil, such as sunflower or vegetable)

4 garlic cloves, finely chopped

about a 2cm (¾in) piece of fresh ginger, grated (shredded); skin on is fine

1 teaspoon garam masala

1 teaspoon dried fenugreek leaves (optional)

½ teaspoon hot chilli powder, or to taste

400g (14oz) tomatoes, finely chopped, or use 1 x 400g (14oz) can of plum tomatoes, chopped

2 tablespoons tomato purée (concentrated paste)

1 teaspoon caster (superfine) sugar

½ teaspoon salt, plus more to season

60ml (2fl oz) double (heavy) cream

freshly ground black pepper

Butter Chicken is a Punjabi curry and traditionally made using two different cooking methods, first by charring the marinated chicken in a tandoor oven until blackened, then by finishing it off in a swath of deeply flavoured sauce made with tomatoes, garlic, ginger, and other spices, of which dry fenugreek leaves are key. Ghee (a generous amount of it) and cream are also elemental to this dish, making it a lavish treat to both cook and eat. It's in the braised chapter because my recipe uses chopped, boneless thigh meat. If you would prefer to char or barbecue the chicken first, then please do. And, of course, use breast meat if you prefer – just cook it for a slightly longer time than if cooking with thighs. Tomatoes shine in this recipe, their sweet acidity a very happy match for all the ghee and cream, and a brilliant combination with the fenugreek, which tastes sweetly nutty and reminiscent of maple syrup.

1. In a bowl mix together the diced chicken with the yogurt, lemon juice and tandoori spice blend and leave to marinate for 1 hour or up to 8 hours.

2. Melt the ghee or butter in a saucepan over a moderate heat. Add the garlic and ginger and fry for 1 minute, until soft and fragrant. Add the garam masala, fenugreek, if using, and chilli and cook for 30 seconds, then add the tomatoes, tomato purée, sugar, salt and 100ml (3½fl oz) of water and cook for 5 minutes, or until the tomatoes have begun to break down, thickening to form a sauce.

3. Add the chicken (including all of the marinade), stirring well and cooking for about 5 minutes over a moderate-high heat until simmering.

4. Cover the pan, turn down the heat to moderate-low and cook for 20-30 minutes, until the chicken is cooked through, and the sauce is rich, thick and deeply flavoured.

5. Stir in half the cream, check the seasoning, then season with salt, pepper and more chilli powder, if necessary. You can also stir in a splash more water if you would like a looser consistency for the sauce. Remove from the heat and let the curry rest for at least 5 minutes before spooning over the remaining cream to serve.

Borscht

2 onions, 1 finely diced, 1 halved
1 bay leaf
3 allspice berries
400g (14oz) diced pork belly, skin
   removed
300g (10½oz) raw, pale-coloured
   beetroot (beet), peeled and coarsely
   grated (shredded)
200g (7oz) floury potatoes, peeled and
   cut into 2cm (¾in) dice
1 tablespoon olive oil, or use a knob
   of butter

1 carrot (about 100g/3½oz), coarsely
   grated (shredded)
1 tablespoon tomato purée
   (concentrated paste)
1 tablespoon cider vinegar, or white or
   red wine vinegar
400g (14oz) ripe tomato, coarsely
   grated (shredded)
100g (3½oz) sauerkraut
salt and freshly ground black pepper
150g (5½oz) sour cream, to serve
½ small bunch of dill, roughly chopped,
   to serve

This is a soup made with tomatoes, grated beetroot and a hearty meat stock (although vegetarian and vegan versions exist, of course, perhaps with added wild mushrooms and without the sour cream). It is richly flavoured, with earthy, sweet notes from the beetroot and tang and acidity by way of tomatoes. The seasons dictate the ingredients that end up in a borscht. Like so many celebrated dishes, there can never be a finite recipe, more like a catalogue of ways and variations to morph. This is a summer borscht, which gives us the ripe tomatoes and fresh dill. Choose beetroots that aren't too deeply purple – the candy, pale-red or pink ones are ideal.

1. Put the halved onion, bay leaf, allspice and diced pork in a saucepan, then add 1.5 litres (52fl oz) of cold water and season generously with salt.

2. Place the pan over a high heat and bring the liquid to a steady simmer, then reduce the heat to a low simmer and cook for 1 hour, occasionally skimming off any residue. After this time, strain the stock, discarding the bay leaf, allspice and onion halves. Put the cooked pork to one side and return the stock to the pan.

3. Add the beetroot and potatoes to the hot stock and cook for 30 minutes over a moderate heat.

4. Meanwhile, heat the oil in a separate pan over a moderate heat. Add the diced onion and grated carrot and cook for about 10 minutes, until the onion is softened.

5. Add the tomato purée and vinegar to the onion and carrot, stirring to combine. Cook for 1 minute, then add the grated tomato and cook for 30 seconds more.

6. Add the tomato and onion mixture and the sauerkraut to the stock, return the cooked pork to the soup and cook for a further 5 minutes or so, until piping hot. Check the seasoning, adding salt and pepper, to taste.

7. Serve the soup in bowls with a big spoonful of sour cream and a sprinkling of dill.

Tomato Ka Salan

2 tablespoons raw, unsalted peanuts, crushed

3 tablespoons desiccated (dried shredded) coconut

½ teaspoon black mustard seeds

½ teaspoon cumin seeds

1 teaspoon sesame seeds

5 curry leaves, fresh or frozen

3 tablespoons coconut oil, ghee or any neutral oil (such as sunflower or vegetable)

1 onion, peeled and finely diced

2 garlic cloves, finely chopped

about a 2cm (¾in) piece of fresh ginger, grated (shredded); skin on is fine

½ teaspoon ground turmeric

1 teaspoon ground coriander

1 teaspoon ground cumin

1–2 teaspoons hot chilli powder

1 tablespoon tamarind pulp

1–3 green chillies, whole or halved lengthways (deseeded if you want less heat)

a pinch of sugar, or to taste

600g (1lb 5oz) tomatoes, halved

50g (1¾oz) full-fat natural (plain) yogurt

salt and freshly ground black pepper

a small bunch of coriander (cilantro), leaves picked and roughly chopped, to serve

I wanted to include a tomato curry from India in this book, and after trying quite a few different methods, this was a favourite, braising the halved tomatoes in the thickened, flavoursome sauce. For this curry, which originates from the Hyderabadi region in south-central India, tomatoes are poached in a sauce of coconut, tamarind, sesame seeds and peanuts. Don't be put off by the long list of ingredients – none is hard to track down, the preparation is simple, and the results are out of this world. My diet on a trip to southern India was mouthwatering – so many different varieties of curry, all served with rice, biriyani or breads and various pickles or chutneys. If you wanted to make the quick tomato chutney (see page 45) to serve alongside, it would be no bad thing.

1. In a deep, dry frying pan over a moderate heat, toast the peanuts for 2 minutes or so, until they begin to just colour, then add the coconut and toast for 30 seconds. Remove from the heat, tip the peanuts and coconut into a food processor and blend with 150ml (5fl oz) water to form a smooth, thin paste.

2. Wipe out the pan and return it to a moderate heat. Add the mustard seeds, cumin seeds, sesame seeds and curry leaves and toast for 1 minute, until they begin to splutter in the pan. Add the coconut oil and the onion, then reduce the heat to moderate–low and cook for about 10 minutes, until the onion has softened.

3. Add the garlic and ginger and cook for 1–2 minutes, until fragrant, then turn the heat back up to moderate. Add the ground spices and cook for 30 seconds, then add the peanut and coconut paste and simmer for 5 minutes, until the oil begins to separate.

4. Add the tamarind, chillies and sugar, and salt to taste, then add the tomatoes, cut side down. Cover and cook for 8–10 minutes, until the tomatoes are soft but not collapsed. Remove from the heat and stir through the yogurt, taking care not to break up the tomatoes. Allow the curry to rest for 5 minutes, then sprinkle with the coriander, to serve.

Tagine

For the chermoula

½ small bunch of coriander (cilantro), leaves picked and roughly chopped

a small bunch of flat-leaf parsley, leaves picked and roughly chopped

3 tablespoons olive oil

juice of ½ lemon

2 garlic cloves, halved

1 small red chilli, roughly chopped (deseeded if you want less heat)

salt and freshly ground black pepper

For the tagine

800g (1lb 12oz) firm, white sustainable fish fillets, cut into bitesize pieces

2 tablespoons olive oil

2 onions, thinly sliced

2 carrots, peeled and thinly sliced

3 garlic cloves, thinly sliced

about a 1cm (½in) piece of fresh ginger, finely grated (shredded); skin on is fine

2 tablespoons tomato purée (concentrated paste)

50g (1¾oz) green olives, pitted

1 teaspoon cumin seeds, toasted and ground

1 teaspoon coriander seeds, toasted and ground

½ teaspoon freshly ground black pepper

1 teaspoon ground turmeric

½ teaspoon salt

300g (10½oz) waxy potatoes, peeled and thinly sliced

1 preserved lemon, skin thinly sliced, flesh discarded, or use ½ unwaxed lemon rind

400g (14oz) tomatoes, thinly sliced

½ small bunch of coriander (cilantro), leaves picked and roughly chopped, to serve

warmed flat breads, to serve

A tagine is the name given to a Moroccan earthenware cooking vessel with a conical lid, but can also refer to the dish itself, a stew made with meat or fish, sometimes pulses, all layered with softened onions, plump, ripe fruits, dried fruits or preserved lemons, and an assortment of North African spices, such as cinnamon, ginger and saffron. I've made a chermoula in this recipe – half to use as a marinade for the fish and the remainder for serving at the table. Crucial to the success of any tagine is the way in which the contents of the dish are put together to cook, layering them to form a near-perfect cooking environment for the flavours to build while maintaining moisture. If you have a tagine for this, great; if not, use a good casserole pan with a tight-fitting lid. This is beautiful cooking, the best of the best.

1. Blend all the ingredients for the chermoula together, season with salt and pepper to taste, then put half in a small serving bowl in the fridge.

2. Tip the fish into a bowl and add the remaining half of the chermoula. Mix them together and leave the fish to marinate for at least 30 minutes or up to 1 hour.

3. Heat the 2 tablespoons of olive oil in a saucepan over a moderate-low heat. Add the onions and carrots and fry for about 10 minutes, until the onion is softened but not coloured.

continued overleaf

4. Turn the heat back up to moderate and add the garlic, ginger, tomato purée, olives and the spices and cook for 30 seconds more. Add the salt and 300ml (10½fl oz) of water and bring the contents of the pan to a gentle simmer. Arrange the potatoes and lemon on top of the sauce in the pan, then top with the sliced tomatoes and drizzle with any chermoula sitting in the bottom of the bowl with the fish. Cover with a lid and simmer over a moderate heat for about 25 minutes, until the potatoes are cooked through and tender.

5. Add the fish to the top of the cooked potatoes in the pan, adding a splash more boiling water if the pan runs the risk of cooking dry – you want a bit of sauce. Cover and simmer gently over a moderate heat for about 10–12 minutes, until the fish is opaque and just cooked through. It will continue to cook a little in the pan after removing it from the heat.

6. To serve, add the chopped coriander and serve immediately, ideally with warm flat breads or couscous.

Tomato and Harissa Mussels

75g (2½oz) butter, cubed and chilled
1 small onion or 2 shallots, thinly sliced
1 fat garlic clove, thinly sliced
200g (7oz) tomatoes, roughly chopped,
  or canned plum tomatoes, chopped,
  or passata
1kg (2lb 4oz) fresh mussels, debearded
  and scrubbed
2 tablespoons harissa paste, or to taste
  (see right for homemade)
1 small bunch of coriander (cilantro),
  leaves picked and roughly chopped
juice of 1 lemon or orange

**For the harissa (makes 1 small jar –
  about 35g/12oz)**
100g (3½oz) long, red chillies (deseeded
  if you want less heat)
200g (7oz) tomatoes
50ml (1¾fl oz) olive oil, plus more to seal
3 garlic cloves, roughly chopped
2 teaspoons cumin seeds, lightly toasted
1 teaspoon caraway seeds, lightly
  toasted
1 teaspoon mild, sweet paprika
1 tablespoon red wine vinegar
salt and freshly ground black pepper

*Mussels are a bivalve, considered to be among the most ethical food choices for the
modern-day diet. Bivalves are sessile, in that they don't move, nor do they require
feeding or agrochemicals to farm, which makes them relatively easy and inexpensive
to produce, with little negative environmental impact. In fact, they filter carbon and
produce no waste, so they really are something of a miracle. They are high-protein and
rich in essential fatty acids and other nutrients, so in all, as a chef and food writer, I see
it as my responsibility to encourage you to buy and cook them. Thankfully, they are also
incredibly delicious. Rinse and debeard the mussels, discarding any that won't close –
to check, just tap them on the side of the sink and the shells should shut tight.*

1. First, make the harissa. Preheat the oven to 210°C/190°C fan/415°F/Gas 6–7.

2. Roast the chillies and the tomatoes for about 15 minutes, turning them halfway
through the cooking time, until blistered and softened. Remove the skin from the
chillies and tomato, and remove the stems from the chillies. (Alternatively, grill/broil
or barbecue them until blackened and blistered.)

3. Blend the skinned tomatoes and chillies with the remaining ingredients to form a
smooth sauce, adding salt and pepper to taste.

4. Spoon the harissa into a clean, sterilized jar, top with a layer of oil, seal the jar and
store the harissa in the fridge until you're ready to use it (it will keep like this for about
1 week).

5. To make the dish, melt half the butter in a pot (with a lid) big enough to fit
everything (remembering that the mussels need lots of space to expand) over
a moderate heat. Add the onion or shallots and fry for about 5–10 minutes, until
softened but not coloured. Add the garlic and cook for 2 minutes, until fragrant.

BRAISED & STOVETOP

continued overleaf

6. Add the tomatoes and cook for about 5 minutes, until rich and thick, then add 150ml (5fl oz) of cold water and bring the liquid to a simmer over a moderate heat.

7. Add the mussels and the harissa to the pan. Cover with a tight-fitting lid and simmer for about 5 minutes, until the mussels open, shaking the pot a couple of times throughout the cook time. Discard any mussels that refuse to open.

8. Remove the pot from the heat and add the coriander, the remaining butter and the citrus juice, stirring well to combine. Serve immediately.

Whole Brisket of Beef Cooked in Tomatoes and Soffritto (for two meals)

1.5kg (3lb 5oz) flat brisket, in one piece
  is ideal
3 tablespoons olive oil
50g (1¾oz) streaky bacon, cut into
  lardons
2 onions, finely diced
2 large carrots, peeled and finely diced
3 celery sticks, finely diced
4 garlic cloves, roughly chopped
2 good-sized sage, thyme or rosemary
  sprigs, leaves picked and finely
  chopped

a small bunch of flat-leaf parsley, leaves
  picked and finely chopped
1 tablespoon tomato purée
  (concentrated paste)
200ml (7fl oz) fruity, rich, dry, red wine
600g (1lb 5oz) passata, or drained
  canned tomatoes, roughly chopped
salt and freshly ground black pepper

An Italian recipe using a large, flat piece of brisket that gets slowly braised in rather a lot of passata, bacon, red wine and soffritto, the classic medley of soft, golden cooked vegetables. What's cleverest of all about this recipe is that you get two complete dishes for the price of one. You serve the brisket with a little of the sauce, perhaps with some thin, roasted potatoes, or even some mash, and then you serve the remainder of the sauce (of which there is plenty) as another meal entirely stirred through some cooked pasta. This recipe is lavish, but also frugal, extolling a thoughtful and sensitive cookery practice, all at the one time, and, in my mind, as near as complete and perfect as cooking can ever get.

1. Try to cook the brisket as a single piece in an ovenproof pan big enough to house it. Otherwise, cut it into 2 or 3 pieces to fit it in the pan.

2. Preheat the oven to 140°C/120°C fan/275°F/Gas 1. Season the brisket all over with salt and pepper.

3. Heat the oil in a saucepan over a high heat and add the brisket, fat-side down. Sear the meat for about 10–15 minutes, until nicely browned on the underside, then carefully flip it over and brown the other side for about 5–10 minutes.

4. Remove the brisket from the pan and put it to one side on a large plate. Next, add the bacon lardons to the pan, reduce the heat to moderate, and cook for about 5 minutes, until the lardons begin to colour.

5. Add all the chopped veg, and the garlic and herbs, and cook over a moderate heat, stirring often, for about 10–15 minutes, until the vegetables are soft, bronzing a little and beginning to stick to the bottom of the pan.

6. Add the tomato purée and the wine to the pan and cook, stirring often, until all the wine has evaporated.

7. Add the passata or tomatoes and bring the liquid to a gentle boil. Season to taste with salt and plenty of pepper.

8. Add the brisket back to the pan on top of all the sauce, cover with a lid and place the pan in the oven for 4–5 hours, until the meat is completely tender and easily pierceable with a fork, but not falling apart. An ideal internal temperature is 90–95°C/194–203°F, and the sauce should be dense and shiny, with a deep, red oil on the surface.

9. Remove the pan from the oven and allow the brisket to rest in the sauce for at least 30 minutes, skimming off some of the excess oil – a little oil is fine, but at this stage there will be rather a lot.

10. Carve the meat and serve it with a spoonful of the sauce per portion. Keep the remainder to serve as a sauce for pasta.

To serve the remaining sauce as a pasta dish

Warm the sauce in a suitable pan. Meanwhile, bring a separate pan of salted water to a boil and add about 300–400g (10½–14oz) of short and shapely pasta to the water (enough for 4 people), cooking it according to the packet instructions until al dente. Drain, reserving a little of the pasta cooking water, and stir the pasta through the warm sauce, loosening with a splash of the reserved water, as necessary. Serve sprinkled with plenty of Parmesan or pecorino.

Baked Tomatoes and Eggs with Basil, Chilli and Parmesan

400g (14oz) tomatoes, large ones
  halved, cherry tomatoes left whole
5 garlic cloves, thinly sliced
½ small bunch of basil, leaves picked and
  roughly chopped
4 tablespoons olive oil, plus more
  for drizzling
3 tablespoons boiling water from a kettle

4 large eggs
½ teaspoon chilli flakes, or to taste
30g (1oz) Parmesan, grated (shredded),
  or to taste
salt and freshly ground black pepper
sliced crusty bread (such as a baguette
  or ciabatta), to serve

This is exactly the sort of breakfast or brunch I would best like to eat after a very late night, probably after a little too much to drink. With morning-after-the-night-before friends still gathered, it is effortless to pull together, looks inviting and demands to be eaten. Best of all, it calls for a lazy trawl of great hunks of bread, blasting through the barely set egg yolks and tomato juices, dripping with abandon. This dish is what makes having a hangover worth it – well, nearly.

1. Preheat the oven to 190°C/170°C fan/375°F/Gas 5.

2. Arrange the tomatoes in a baking dish of about 20 x 30cm (8 x 12in). Tuck the garlic in among the tomatoes, add three-quarters of the basil, then the olive oil and boiling water. Season well with salt and pepper.

3. Bake the tomatoes, uncovered, for about 20 minutes, until they have softened, slumping into a sauce, of sorts.

4. Remove the dish from the oven and tease 4 pockets into the surface area of the tomatoes (using the back of a spoon), cracking an egg into each. Season the eggs and turn up the heat to 220°C/200°C fan/425°F/Gas 7.

5. Cover and return the dish to the oven and bake for about 8–10 minutes, until the egg whites are opaque but the yolks are still runny.

6. Remove the dish from the oven, scatter over the remaining basil and the chilli flakes and Parmesan. Drizzle with a little extra olive oil, if you like, and serve with good bread.

BRAISED & STOVETOP

Saffron Rice with Roasted Tomatoes, Prawns and Aïoli

4 tablespoons olive oil

1 onion, finely diced

1 red (bell) pepper, deseeded and finely diced

3 garlic cloves, finely chopped

2 tablespoons tomato purée (concentrated paste)

200g (7oz) paella rice

1 litre (35fl oz) hot chicken or vegetable stock

a good-sized pinch of saffron, steeped in 2 tablespoons boiling water (optional, but recommended)

2 bay leaves, scrunched a little

400g (14oz) tomatoes, roughly chopped, or 1 x 400g (14oz) can of plum tomatoes, chopped

450g (1lb) frozen prawns (shrimp), defrosted

For the aïoli

2 large egg yolks

a good pinch of salt, plus more to taste

4-6 garlic cloves, to taste, mashed with a little salt to form a paste

450ml (16fl oz) sunflower or vegetable oil (or use half and half with good olive oil)

splash of red wine vinegar, to taste

freshly ground black pepper

To serve

a small bunch of flat-leaf parsley, leaves picked and finely chopped

½ small bunch of tarragon, chervil or chives, finely chopped

1 lemon or orange, cut into wedges

This is a decadent lunch or dinner to eat outside with the sun on your back, ideally in sight of the sea. Essentially, you're making a pilaf, the steamed rice glinting gold and red with saffron and peppers, which you then stir through with roasted tomatoes, prawns and some of the aïoli. Choose responsibly sourced prawns, although you could omit them, if you like, sticking with just the tomatoes.

1. First, make the aïoli (this method is by hand, but you can use a small food processor to bring the mayonnaise together, if you have one). In a bowl (or the bowl of a small food processor), whisk together the egg yolks with the salt and garlic paste.

2. Put the oil in a jug that is easy to pour from, then slowly start whisking a few drops of oil at a time into the egg mixture.

3. Gradually increase the quantity of oil you add each time, whisking in each addition so that it is properly amalgamated before adding any more. Once the mayonnaise begins to hold its shape, you can start to add the oil in a steady, thin stream. When you have added all the oil, you should have a thick and wobbly mayonnaise that holds its shape easily.

4. Taste and check the seasoning, adding more salt if you think it needs it – some pepper is good too – then add a splash of vinegar to taste. The aïoli should be highly seasoned. Set aside while you prepare the dish.

continued overleaf

5. Preheat the oven to 180°C/160°C fan/350°F/Gas 4.

6. Heat half the olive oil in a pan over a moderate heat. Add the onion and the pepper and fry for about 10 minutes, until the onion is soft but not coloured. Add the garlic, tomato purée and rice, stirring well to toast the rice until it is translucent at the edges and well tinged with the tomato purée. Cook for about 1 minute over a moderate heat.

7. Add the stock, saffron and saffron soaking water (if using) and bay leaves. Bring the contents of the pan to a rapid simmer. Cover and put the dish in the oven to cook for about 20-25 minutes, until the rice is tender.

8. While the rice is cooking, add the tomatoes to a baking dish and season well with salt and pepper, then add the remaining olive oil. Bake, uncovered, in the oven for about 10-15 minutes to soften slightly. Add the prawns and cook for a further 5 minutes, until the prawns are opaque and just cooked through. Remove the tomato dish from the oven and put it to one side.

9. When the rice is cooked, add the roasted tomatoes and prawns, including all the juices, and stir gently to combine. Then, add about 3 heaped tablespoons of the aïoli, again stirring gently to combine. Let the dish sit for 5 minutes before serving.

10. Scatter over the chopped herbs and serve with the remaining aïoli and the lemon or orange wedges at the table.

Groundnut Stew

700g (1lb 9oz) bone-in, skinless chicken
  thighs
3 tablespoons sunflower, vegetable
  or coconut oil, plus more to cook
  the plantain
1 large onion, finely sliced
4cm (1½in) piece of fresh ginger, grated
  (shredded); skin on is fine
2 garlic cloves, finely chopped
1–3 teaspoons chilli flakes or 1–2 fresh
  chopped red or green chillies, to taste
1 teaspoon freshly ground black pepper,
  plus more to season
2 tablespoons tomato purée
  (concentrated paste)
400g (14oz) tomatoes, roughly chopped,
  or 1 x 400g (14oz) can of plum
  tomatoes, chopped

200g (7oz) smooth, unsweetened
  peanut butter
600ml (21fl oz) chicken stock or water
salt

To serve
1 plantain, peeled and cut into 2cm
  (¾in) slices
200g (7oz) tomatoes, roughly chopped
1–3 red chillies (I like Scotch Bonnet),
  finely sliced
50g (1¾oz) roasted, salted peanuts,
  roughly chopped
a small bunch of coriander (cilantro),
  leaves picked and roughly chopped
2 hard-boiled eggs, sliced

*My mum grew up for some time in Sierra Leone. Her stories make my children's eyes
pop with wonder – my mum saving her younger sister from being swept away to sea
by pulling hard on her ponytail; bumpy, middle-of-the-night trips through the jungle
in a reconvened lorry; monkeys and baboons on the front doorstep; crocodiles in the
mangroves; and leopards on the way to school. There is also this stew, which my mum
loved so much that she cooked it often for my brother and me, far from Sierra Leone in
1980s London. She served it then with banana, my British-born friends round for tea
finding this most intriguing of all. These days, my children clamour for it whenever we
visit. I now find plantain fairly easy to come by – choose a ripe, black speckled fruit.*

1. Season the chicken all over with salt and pepper.

2. Heat the oil in a large saucepan over a moderate-high heat and add the chicken to
the pan. Seal the chicken thighs on both sides, working in batches if you need to. Once
the thighs are gently browned all over, remove them from the pan and set them to
one side on a plate.

3. Add three-quarters of the onion to the pan, turn down the heat to moderate and
cook for about 5 minutes, until softened a little, then add the ginger, garlic and chilli
and cook for a further 8–10 minutes, until softened.

4. Add the black pepper and the tomato purée and cook for about 2–3 minutes,
stirring, until everything begins to lightly caramelize.

continued overleaf

5. Add the tomatoes and cook for about 10 minutes to thicken a little. Stir in the peanut butter and return the chicken thighs to the pan, along with the stock or water. Bring the liquid to a boil, reduce the heat to moderate-low and cook, covered, for about 45 minutes–1 hour, until the chicken is cooked through and tender.

6. Remove the pan from the heat, check the seasoning, adding more salt and a generous amount of black pepper where necessary.

7. In a frying pan, add a spot of oil and place the pan over a moderate heat. Add the plantain and fry for about 2–3 minutes, turning halfway through, until lightly caramelized all over (work in batches if you need to). Remove from the heat and put to one side.

8. Sprinkle the remaining onion with a little salt, to soften.

9. Serve the groundnut stew with the chopped tomatoes, salted onion, fresh chillies, crushed peanuts, fried plantain, chopped coriander and hard-boiled eggs.

Tomato and Saffron Risotto

500g (1lb 2oz) tomatoes
3 tablespoons olive oil
3 shallots, finely diced
3 garlic cloves, finely chopped
2 thyme sprigs, leaves picked
350g (12oz) arborio or carnaroli
  risotto rice
150ml (5fl oz) dry white wine
a pinch of saffron, steeped in
  2 tablespoons boiling water

1 teaspoon salt, plus more to season
1 litre (35fl oz) hot chicken or vegetable
  stock
30g (1oz) butter
80g (2¾oz) Parmesan or pecorino,
  grated (shredded)
freshly ground black pepper

I am very bossy when it comes to making risotto. Perhaps partly because I have seen served, and been served, too many solid mounds of rice masquerading as risotto. Risotto should glide across the plate if you tilt it from one side to the other. The rice should be suspended in a glossy, creamy viscous liquid, a liquid that has had no cream added, rather butter and Parmesan or pecorino beaten in at the end, emulsifying with the stock. The grains of rice should be tender, with a slight bite to the very centre, remembering it will need a good, long rest before serving and so will continue to cook a little in the residual heat. Peeling the tomatoes for this recipe is absolutely worth it, giving you tender chunks that almost melt during the cook time. I'd urge to make twice this quantity, giving you the requisite leftovers to make arancini (see page 133). Original recipe published by The Tomato Stall (@iowtomatoes) and reprinted here with their kind permission.

1. To prepare the tomatoes, have a large pan of boiling water ready. Slash each tomato with a sharp knife and plunge them into boiling water for 10 seconds (in batches if needed). Remove them with a slotted spoon and put to one side until cool enough to handle - after which, the skin should slip off easily (plunge for 5 seconds more if not). Remove the tough cores then roughly dice the flesh, seeds and all. Put to one side.

2. Heat the oil in a large saucepan over a moderate heat. Add the shallots and fry for 3 minutes, until softened but not coloured. Add the garlic and thyme, then add the rice and stir for a minute so the rice grains go slightly milky and translucent at the edges. Add the wine, and the saffron and its soaking water, and stir briskly until all the liquid has been absorbed. Add the tomatoes and salt and stir well for 1 minute more.

3. Reduce the heat to moderate-low and add the stock, a ladleful at a time, ensuring each is absorbed before adding more. You should need to use all the stock, but risotto rice does vary in absorbency, so do check it from about 15 minutes onward - it's ready when tender but with a slight bite to the very centre of each grain. If it's not ready, continue cooking for 5-10 minutes more. Remember the rice will continue cooking in the residual heat once you've put it to one side to rest (which it must do sufficiently).

4. To finish, beat in the butter and half the Parmesan or pecorino. Season with salt and plenty of pepper, cover and set aside for 5 minutes before serving with more cheese.

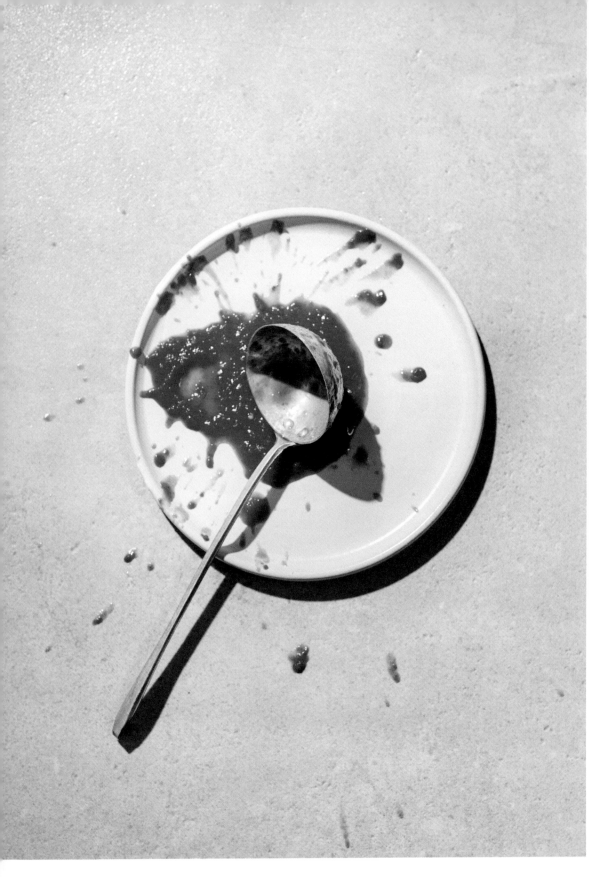

Tomatoes and Courgettes with Chickpeas and Olive Oil

600g (1lb 5oz) courgettes (zucchini),
  sliced into 5mm (¼in) rounds
4 garlic cloves, thinly sliced
4 tablespoons olive oil, plus more
  to serve
1 onion, thinly sliced
500g (1lb 2oz) tomatoes, roughly
  chopped, or 2 x 400g (14oz) cans of
  plum tomatoes, chopped

2 x 400g (14oz) cans of chickpeas,
  drained and rinsed
a big bunch of parsley or basil, leaves
  picked and roughly chopped
salt and freshly ground black pepper

The stark simplicity of this recipe means there is nowhere to hide. You will need to maximize flavour in the way you cook this, sensitively and with assurance, from the off. This is a classic way to cook tomatoes with additional vegetables, slowly and thoughtfully, altering character, unifying, but also still allowing for each ingredient to still be very much of its own. Using so few ingredients, while achieving a highly delicious result, will give you confidence as a cook. So, I will say this (even though we're over halfway through a cookbook about tomatoes), use the best-quality, ripest and sweetest tomatoes you can get your hands on. Failing that, use the very best cans your budget affords. Choose firm, small courgettes, which will maintain shape, despite the substantial cook time, and deliver the best flavour. Large courgettes will cook to a mush.

1. Preheat the oven to 210°C/190°C fan/415°F/Gas 6–7.

2. Toss the courgettes and garlic with 2 tablespoons of the olive oil and roast them in a deep baking dish for 15–20 minutes, until the courgettes are soft and beginning to colour. Remove from the oven.

3. While the courgettes are roasting, heat the remaining oil in a pan over a moderate heat. Add the onion and fry for about 10 minutes, until softened but not coloured. Add the tomatoes to the pan and cook for about 10 minutes to thicken.

4. Add the chickpeas and half the parsley or basil and stir to combine, fully warming through. Add the courgettes, seasoning well with salt and pepper. Remove from the heat and cool a little.

5. Serve the dish warm or at room temperature with the remaining parsley or basil scattered over and a drizzle more olive oil.

Tomato, Lamb and Black Olive Ragù with Gremolata

800g (1lb 12oz) diced lamb shoulder
3 tablespoons olive oil
1 large onion, finely diced
2 celery sticks, finely diced
2 small carrots, peeled and finely diced
4 garlic cloves, finely chopped
4-6 thyme sprigs, leaves picked
2 bay leaves, scrunched a little
scant 1 teaspoon ground fennel
1 x 400g (14oz) can of plum tomatoes, chopped, or 400g (14oz) fresh tomatoes, peeled and roughly chopped

300ml (10½fl oz) chicken or lamb stock or water
50g (1¾oz) best-quality black or kalamata olives, pitted
400g (14oz) pasta of choice
salt and freshly ground black pepper

For the gremolata
finely grated zest of ½ lemon
a small bunch of flat-leaf parsley, very finely chopped
1 garlic clove, very finely chopped

Tomatoes are many things to many people. In a casserole such as this one, they make for a most sublime sauce in which to cook the lamb until tender, almost to the point of falling apart (but not quite). I've added bay, thyme and olives to this casserole and served it with some pasta. I've also made a gremolata – parsley, lemon and garlic all very finely chopped, then showered over the finished dish to serve. This is a recipe with low, slow, soft and sweet base notes, the gremolata thundering in, a flashy finish, full of pep. If you prefer, you can use chicken or beef instead of the lamb.

1. Preheat the oven to 140°C/120°C fan/275°F/Gas 1. Season the lamb all over.

2. Heat the oil in a casserole or ovenproof saucepan over a moderate–high heat until very hot. Add the lamb and cook, turning occasionally, for about 3-5 minutes, until browned. Remove the lamb from the pan and put it to one side on a plate.

3. Add the onion, celery and carrots to the pan, turn down the heat to moderate, and sauté for about 10-12 minutes, until the onion has softened and the vegetables are just beginning to caramelize. Add the garlic and fry for 2 minutes, until fragrant. Add the thyme leaves, bay leaves and ground fennel, then add the tomatoes and stock and bring the liquid to a boil.

4. Return the browned lamb to the pan, then cover and place the pan in the oven. Bake for 1-2 hours, until the lamb is tender, melting and almost falling apart in pieces.

5. Remove the pan from the oven, add the olives and check the seasoning, adjusting with salt and pepper, if necessary.

6. Allow the ragù to rest for 10 minutes while you boil the pasta in a pan of well-salted water according to the packet instructions, until tender. Meanwhile, prepare the gremolata by mixing together the lemon zest, parsley and garlic, stirring well to combine.

7. To serve, spoon cooked pasta into a bowl, add the lamb ragù and a generous scattering of gremolata.

Tomato and Beef Stew with Black Beans and Ancho Chilli with Fried Tortilla

1 teaspoon ground cumin

¼ teaspoon ground allspice

¼ teaspoon ground cinnamon

a pinch of ground cloves

1 teaspoon salt, plus more to season

1kg (2lb 4oz) diced beef shin, ox cheeks cut in quarters, or stewing steak

6 tomatoes (about 600g/1lb 5oz)

4 garlic cloves, skin on

1 small onion, cut into 6 wedges, core intact

2 ancho or pasilla chillies, deseeded

1 tablespoon lard (clarified pork fat), dripping or vegetable oil, plus extra for frying the tortilla

1 tablespoon pumpkin seeds

1 teaspoon red wine vinegar

1 teaspoon sugar or runny honey

2 bay leaves, scrunched a little

1 x 400g (14oz) can of black beans, drained

salt and freshly ground black pepper

To serve

soft corn or wheat tortillas, sliced into triangles

1 avocado, stoned and sliced

burnt tomato salsa (see page 32)

½ red onion, finely sliced and soaked in boiling water for 5 minutes, drained and seasoned with a big pinch of salt

hot sauce (see page 25 for homemade)

Try to source ancho or pasilla chilli for this recipe – online or larger supermarkets should do it. Ancho chillies have a mild and fruity flavour, especially suited to tomatoes. Burning the tomatoes, whole garlic and chillies until the tomato skins blacken and blister, the garlic sort of implodes and the chilli is aromatic, is crucial, helping to ramp up the flavour from the get-go. Ideally you would use beef shin or cheeks for premium melt-in-the-mouth texture, but stewing steak would do. If you don't want to fry your own tortillas, feel free to use shop-bought tortilla chips.

1. Combine half of each of the ground spices with the teaspoon of salt in a bowl and rub the mixture into the beef. Leave to marinate for 1 hour, or overnight in the fridge.

2. Preheat the oven to 140°C/120°C fan/275°F/Gas 1.

3. Heat a frying pan over a high heat. Add the tomatoes, garlic cloves and onion wedges and dry-fry for about 10 minutes, turning every now and then, until well blistered and charred. Remove the pan from the heat and put the tomatoes, garlic cloves and onion wedges to one side. Dry-fry the chillies in the same pan, for about 2 minutes, until toasted and fragrant. Remove from the heat.

4. Remove the skins from the tomatoes and garlic and blitz them with the onions and chillies to form a smooth purée. Put to one side.

5. Heat the lard, dripping or oil in a casserole over a moderate–high heat. Add the marinated beef and seal for 5–10 minutes, until nicely coloured. Remove the meat from the pan using a slotted spoon and set it to one side. Reserve the fat in the pan.

BRAISED & STOVETOP

continued overleaf

6. Add the tomato and garlic purée to the pan and cook for 2–3 minutes, then add the remaining ingredients except the beans, including the remaining spices, and cook for 10 minutes, until the sauce is thick, seasoning with salt and pepper to taste.

7. Return the browned beef to the pan and add enough water to almost cover. Cover the pan and place it in the oven for about 2–3 hours, until the beef is tender, almost falling apart. You may need to top up with a little splash of water during the cooking time if the liquid dries out too much – you want a bit of a sauce.

8. Remove the pan from the oven, add the beans, stirring to combine, then rest the stew for about 10 minutes. Pull the meat into large shreds and season well with salt and pepper. Keep warm.

9. To serve, fry the tortillas in a splash of oil in a non-stick or cast-iron pan until crisp and golden and serve them alongside the beef stew, with slices of avocado, the burnt tomato salsa, the red onions and the hot sauce.

Tomatoes Cooked with Sausages and Red Wine

80g (2¾oz) butter
8 good-quality, meaty sausages
  per person
3 garlic cloves, finely chopped
8 sage leaves, finely chopped
2 bay leaves, scrunched a little
½ teaspoon chilli flakes, plus more
  to taste
1 tablespoon tomato purée
  (concentrated paste)

150ml (5fl oz) full-bodied, dry red wine
1 x 400g (14oz) can of plum tomatoes,
  roughly chopped
1 litre (35fl oz) chicken stock or water
120g (4¼oz) fast-cook polenta
80g (2¾oz) Parmesan, grated
  (shredded)
salt and freshly ground black pepper

Because you're braising the sausages in the tomatoes and red wine for this recipe, choose a good, meaty sausage (ideally Italian) that will cook firm, ultimately tenderizing in the sauce. A sausage with too much rusk or oats will turn mealy in the cooking juices, which is a bit unappealing (although fine for a simple sausage-in-a-bun-type scenario). I've given the method for quick-cook polenta here, because it's this polenta that seems to be most commonly available in the UK. Please do feel free to use proper polenta, if you prefer, bearing in mind the longer cook time, should you wish to.

1. Melt half the butter in a frying pan over a moderate heat. Add the sausages and fry, turning occasionally, for 5 minutes, until nicely browned but not cooked through. Transfer the sausages to a plate, reserving the drippings in the pan.

2. Add the garlic, herbs and chilli flakes and cook them in the pan with the drippings for about 2 minutes, until the garlic is fragrant. Add the tomato purée and cook for 30 seconds more, then add the red wine and cook over a moderate–high heat for 5 minutes, until rich and thick.

3. Add the tomatoes, season with salt and pepper and turn down the heat to moderate. Cook the tomatoes for 15 minutes, until thickened.

4. Pour the stock or salted water into a large saucepan, place it over a high heat and bring it to a boil. Whisk in the polenta, add a teaspoon of salt and reduce the heat to low. Simmer, stirring often, for about 10–15 minutes, until thick and the polenta is cooked out, soft and voluptuous, and not gritty in the slightest. Add the remaining butter and three-quarters of the Parmesan, stirring to combine. Remove from the heat and keep warm.

5. While the polenta is cooking, return the sausages to the pan of tomatoes and cook over a moderate heat for about 10 minutes, until the sausages are cooked through. Check the seasoning, adding more salt and pepper if needed. Remove from the heat.

6. To serve, spoon some polenta on to a plate or into a wide bowl and top with the sausages, adding the remaining Parmesan, and more chilli flakes, to taste.

BRAISED & STOVETOP

As we've seen already, heat does marvellous things for tomatoes. From loaves to tarts and pies, in this chapter, the dry heat of roasting and baking incinerates the tomato skins, combusting the flesh within, drawing moisture, distilling flavour and further intensifying the sweet and fragrant character. I love to bake bread, and baking tomatoes (I find cherry are best for this purpose) into a loaf is a winning combination – pressed into a focaccia, drenched in olive oil, turning the crust sublime, with a much-vaunted chewiness; or squashed into the surface of a soda bread to bake, with grated cheese, scone-like in texture, to eat slathered with butter and more tomatoes, this time sliced. There is also a lasagne in this chapter – no meat, just best-quality canned cherry tomatoes cooked down as a sauce, with béchamel, mozzarella and Parmesan, the soft and oozy folds of red and white best eaten warm, never piping hot. There are 12 recipes in total here, so it's probably about time that I told you to get the oven on.

Baked & Roasted

Tomato Focaccia

330ml lukewarm water
7g (⅙oz) fast-action dried yeast
500g (1lb 2oz) strong white bread flour
6 tablespoons olive oil, plus extra for
 greasing
1 teaspoon salt

200g (7oz) cherry tomatoes, some
 halved, some not
about 8 sage leaves; or 3 rosemary
 sprigs, torn
generous ½ teaspoon flaky sea salt

This needs no introduction – it is as much a joy to bake as it is to eat. Use cherry tomatoes for optimum results – sliced tomatoes will work, but you won't get juicy little planets of blistered and sweet tomatoes pockmarking the surface of the bread, some sinking into the doughy dimples, and some not.

1. Stir together the water and yeast and leave it to sit for 5–10 minutes, until foamy.

2. Tip the flour into a large mixing bowl or the bowl of a stand mixer. Add the yeast mixture, mixing vigorously, either by hand or using the dough hook, for a minute or so, then add 2 tablespoons of the olive oil and the teaspoon of salt. Continue mixing for about 10 minutes, until the dough becomes less sticky, smoother and more cohesive.

3. Brush a bowl with olive oil and tip in the dough. Cover and leave the dough to rise in a warm place for about 1–1½ hours, until it has nearly doubled in size.

4. Brush a deep-sided baking pan with a little olive oil, then tip the risen dough into the pan. Pull the dough into shape, towards the edges of the pan, and use your fingertips to dimple it in places, keeping some spots still nicely aerated. Add about 1 tablespoon more of the olive oil over the surface of the dough, cover and leave to prove for 20 minutes.

5. Preheat the oven to 230°C/210°C fan/415°F/Gas 6–7.

6. Add the cherry tomatoes to the dough, squeezing some deep into pockets and leaving some protruding out a little more. Do the same with the sage leaves or torn rosemary sprigs. Sprinkle over the flaky sea salt.

7. Bake the dough in the very hot oven for about 25 minutes, until the crust is golden brown and puffed around edges. The loaf should sound hollow when tapped on the underside.

8. Remove the focaccia from the oven and immediately drench it with the remaining olive oil, then allow it to cool for at least 10–15 minutes before slicing.

Tomato and Cheddar Soda Bread

375g (13oz) plain (all-purpose) flour, plus extra for dusting
1 teaspoon bicarbonate of soda (baking soda)
1 teaspoon salt
½ small bunch of chives, chopped
about ½ teaspoon freshly ground black pepper

80g (2¾oz) cheddar, grated (shredded)
300ml (10½fl oz) buttermilk, or natural (plain) yogurt thinned with a little milk
1 teaspoon Dijon mustard
6–8 sundried tomatoes (smoked are good), finely chopped
10 cherry tomatoes, halved

This is a double whammy, a home run, for tomatoes. I'm a big fan of sundried tomatoes, tasting as they do exaggerated and so intensely of tomato. Used in this soda bread, they are a wonderful, candy-sweet foil for the sharp buttermilk. Soda bread requires little or no kneading, just enough to swiftly bring the dough together as one gnarled and cohesive mass, which you then drop into a tin, in this case stud with tomatoes, and then bake until golden.

1. Preheat the oven to 200°C/180°C fan/400°F/Gas 6. Line a baking sheet with baking paper.

2. Tip the flour, bicarbonate of soda, salt, chives and black pepper into a mixing bowl.

3. In a jug, stir together the cheese with the buttermilk or yogurt, the mustard and sundried tomatoes. Mix well to combine.

4. Swiftly add the wet mixture to the dry mixture and combine them with a fork. Do not over-mix the dough – it should be a cohesive, sticky mass, just holding together. Tip the dough out on to a flour-dusted surface and shape it into a rough-hewn loaf, about 35 x 10cm (14 x 4in).

5. Place the loaf on the lined baking sheet and use a very sharp knife to slash it deeply 3 times across the top. Dot the top of the loaf with the fresh tomatoes, pushing some partially into the dough, and leaving some to protrude a little more.

6. Dust with a little extra flour and bake the loaf for 35–40 minutes, until a skewer inserted into the centre comes out clean and the loaf sounds hollow when tapped from beneath.

7. Remove the loaf from the oven and cool it on a wire rack for at least 15 minutes before slicing.

Tomato Bread and Butter Pudding with Ricotta and Mustard

2 tablespoons Dijon mustard, plus more
  to serve
60g (2oz) butter, softened, plus more
  to grease the dish
about 200g (7oz) day-old focaccia or
  baguette, thinly sliced
250g (9oz) ricotta
350ml (12fl oz) whole milk
300ml (10½fl oz) double (heavy) cream

about 8 sage leaves, chopped, or
  ½ small bunch of chives, thyme or
  oregano, leaves picked as relevant and
  finely chopped
5 eggs, beaten
400g (14oz) cherry tomatoes, halved
80g (2¾oz) cheddar, gruyère or comté,
  coarsely grated (shredded)
salt and freshly ground black pepper

If daubing day-old focaccia with a mustard butter on the one side and thick clouds of ricotta on the other, then baking with an egg custard all dotted with cherry tomatoes and sage leaves sounds up your street, then this is the recipe for you. Serve it warm, never piping hot, for the flavours to fuse and the different components to settle and slump all together, as one. A green salad, dressed with a light vinaigrette, or some steamed vegetables (green beans would be nice), make a fine serving suggestion to compensate for all the dairy. Original recipe published by The Tomato Stall (@iowtomatoes) and reprinted here with their kind permission.

1. Preheat the oven to 165°C/145°C fan/320°F/Gas 2–3 and butter a 25cm (10in) baking dish.

2. In a bowl, beat together the mustard and the butter.

3. Butter the slices of bread on one side with the mustard butter. On the other side, spread each with a layer of ricotta. Arrange the bread, buttered side up, in overlapping rows to fill the dish.

4. In a mixing bowl, whisk the milk, cream, herbs and eggs and season well with plenty of freshly ground black pepper and a good pinch or two of salt. Pour this mixture over the bread and leave the dish for 15 minutes.

5. Add the tomatoes evenly over the top, then sprinkle over the cheese. Bake for 40–45 minutes, until the custard is set, but still a bit wobbly in the centre of the dish, the top golden brown and the sides bubbling.

6. Remove from the oven and leave to rest for 10–15 minutes before serving with extra Dijon on the side, if you like.

Tomato, Crab and Shallot Tart

350g (12oz) shortcrust pastry
  (shop-bought or homemade)
300g (10½oz) cherry or small tomatoes,
  halved
3 tablespoons olive oil
3 shallots, thinly sliced

2 large eggs, plus 1 egg yolk
150ml (5fl oz) double (heavy) cream
a small bunch of chives, chopped
150g (5½oz) picked white or brown
  crab (it's up to you which)
salt and freshly ground black pepper

Tomato and crab complement each other beautifully. Both are sweet in character, one with a perfumed acidity, the other with a pleasing brininess. Here, they're baked in a pastry case with shallots (sweet and nutty when roasted), and topped with a delicate egg custard. This is an elegant, rich dish that delivers beautifully with layers of flavour. Eat it warm or cold with a green salad (watercress would be ideal), and a glass of something minerally and delicious wine-wise.

1. Preheat the oven to 200°C/180°C fan/400°F/Gas 6.

2. Remove the pastry from the fridge and roll it out to a circle about 24cm (11½in) in diameter. Place over a 20cm (8in) tart case and leave it to sink into the hollow. Press it into the base with your fingertips and push it up the sides and into the corners, making the base and corners as thin as possible and leaving no gaps or holes. Trim the edge to neaten.

3. Line the base with baking paper and some baking beans (pie weights) or rice. Leave the pastry case to rest in the fridge for 30 minutes.

4. Meanwhile, lay the tomatoes, cut-side up, in a roasting tin and sprinkle them with salt and half the olive oil. Roast for 10–15 minutes, until slightly softened and caramelized.

5. Bake the chilled pastry case for 10 minutes, until firm but not coloured, then remove the baking beans or rice and baking paper and return the pastry case to the oven for 12–15 minutes, until cooked through and golden.

6. While the tart case is baking, heat the remaining oil in a frying pan over a medium heat. Add the shallots and fry for about 8 minutes, until soft, then put to one side.

7. In a bowl, beat together the eggs, egg yolk and cream until fully combined. Add the cooked shallots and season to taste with salt and pepper.

8. Pour this mixture into the cooked pastry case, top with the roasted tomatoes, cut-side up, then scatter over the chives and crab in an even layer. Season with lots of black pepper and return the tart to the oven.

9. Turn the heat down to 180°C/160°C fan/350°F/Gas 4 and cook for about 20–25 minutes, or until the custard is mostly set, with a small wobble in the middle.

10. Leave the tart to cool a little in the tin, then slide it out on to a plate or board and slice to serve.

BAKED & ROASTED

Palermo Pizza

For the dough
280ml (9¾fl oz) lukewarm water
7g (⅙oz) fast-action dried yeast
500g (1lb 2oz) strong white bread flour
1 teaspoon salt

For the sauce
4 tablespoons olive oil, plus more
  to drizzle
3 onions, thinly sliced
2 garlic cloves, thinly sliced
600g (1lb 5oz) canned plum tomatoes,
  drained and roughly chopped, or

600g (1lb 5oz) peeled fresh tomatoes,
  roughly chopped
salt and freshly ground black pepper

For the topping
6 sundried tomatoes, finely chopped;
  or 6 anchovy fillets, drained and finely
  chopped
1 teaspoon dried oregano
100g (3½oz) pecorino, coarsely grated
  (shredded), or use Parmesan at a push
60g (2oz) fresh breadcrumbs

I spotted this style of pizza at the train station in Palermo in Sicily. Sold in thickset squares stuffed in paper bags, this was to be the train picnic of dreams. Bright red with tomato sauce and glossy with olive oil, the pizza was topped with breadcrumbs, which was a bit of an anomaly for me – but how wrong I was. Breadcrumbs, fried until golden and crunchy and seasoned well with salt are a commonplace addition to finishing foods, especially so in southern Italy and Sicily, a practice derived from the band of cookery known as cucina povera, *or food of the poor. On a pizza, they are, quite frankly, a must-have, mind-blowing addition. Thank you to the vendor at Palermo station – this is my tribute to you.*

1. Make the dough. In a bowl, stir together the water and yeast and leave it to sit for 10–15 minutes, until foamy. Tip the flour into the bowl of a stand mixer fitted with a dough hook (or do this by hand). Add the yeast mixture and mix for at least 5 minutes (if you're doing this by hand, mix for 3–5 minutes longer). Add the salt and continue to mix for 3 minutes (by either method), until smooth. Cover and set aside for 1 hour, until it has doubled in size.

2. Meanwhile, make the sauce. Heat 3 tablespoons of the oil in a pan over a moderate-low heat. Add the onions and fry for about 10–15 minutes, until very soft and rich-tasting, but not coloured. Add the garlic and cook for 1 minute more, then add the tomatoes, seasoning well with salt and pepper. Cook for 15 minutes, until rich and thick.

3. Preheat the oven to 200°C/180°C fan/400°F/Gas 6 and line a 40 x 30cm (16 x 12in) baking sheet with baking paper. Grease it with the remaining 1 tablespoon of olive oil.

4. Lightly flour the work surface and roll out the dough to fit the tray - it should be about 5mm (¼in) thick. Scatter the sundried tomatoes and the oregano over the top.

5. Make a small lip around the edge of the dough, to work as a barrier for the tomato sauce, and spoon the sauce over, spreading it out to the edges. Sprinkle the pecorino or Parmesan over the top, then the breadcrumbs, and drizzle with olive oil.

6. Cook the pizza for 18-25 minutes, until the top is nicely coloured and the base is crisp beneath. Remove from the oven and cut into sizeable (train picnic!) squares.

Tomato and Goat's Cheese Galette

30g (1oz) butter
3 shallots or 1 onion, thinly sliced
3 thyme sprigs, leaves picked and
  chopped
plain (all-purpose) flour, for dusting
300g (10½oz) shortcrust pastry
50g (1¾oz) Parmesan or another hard
  cheese, grated (shredded)

150g (5½oz) soft goat's cheese
350g (12oz) tomatoes, thinly sliced
  (a mixture of colours and sizes is nice)
olive oil, for drizzling
pinch of caster (superfine) sugar
1 egg, beaten, to glaze
salt and freshly ground black pepper

If you use shop-bought shortcrust pastry, then this galette really is a doddle to make for a quick midweek lunch or dinner. Layering the pastry with a dusting of Parmesan is unbeatable. Free-form, baked not in a tin, but on a baking sheet, the real beauty of a galette isn't precision, but insouciance – a tart made to look very natural and artful in its casual, thrown-together appearance.

1. Melt the butter in a pan over a moderate heat. Add the shallots or onion, season well with salt and pepper and fry for about 5–10 minutes (depending on whether you're using shallots or onions), until soft and just beginning to brown. Remove from the heat and stir in the thyme. Put to one side to cool.

2. Lightly flour a work surface and roll out the dough to a rough rectangle about 3mm (⅛in) thick. Sprinkle with the Parmesan, then fold the pastry over itself four times to create four layers of cheese. Wrap the pastry in baking paper and refrigerate for about 10–15 minutes, to rest.

3. Preheat the oven to 190°C/170°C fan/325°F/Gas 3.

4. Lightly flour your work surface and roll out the chilled pastry to a rough circle about 28cm (11¼in) in diameter and about 3mm (⅛in) thick.

5. Transfer the pastry circle to a baking sheet lined with baking paper and coarsely grind black pepper over the top, giving it a final roll to press the pepper into the dough.

6. Add the cooked shallot or onion in an even layer, leaving a 4cm (1½in) border around the edge. Sprinkle the topping with salt and pepper and dot most of the goat's cheese over the top.

7. Add the tomato slices and drizzle with olive oil, sprinkle over the sugar and season with salt, then dot over the rest of the goat's cheese. Fold the edge of the dough over the tomatoes to create a 4cm (1½in) crust.

8. Brush the crust edge with the beaten egg and put the tart in the fridge for 15 minutes to rest.

9. Bake the galette for 40–50 minutes, until the pastry is crisp and golden and the tomatoes are very soft and starting to colour.

10. Remove from the oven and allow to cool for 5 minutes before serving.

Sicilian Timballo di Anelletti

1 large aubergine (eggplant), cut into
 1cm (½in) pieces
500g (1lb 2oz) tomatoes, roughly
 chopped; or 500g (1lb 2oz) cherry
 tomatoes, halved
6 tablespoons olive oil
1 onion, finely diced
2-3 garlic cloves, finely chopped
1 teaspoon dried oregano
400g (14oz) passata
400g (14oz) anelli or macaroni

80g (2¾oz) pecorino or Parmesan,
 grated (shredded), plus more to serve
40g (1½oz) panko or other dried
 breadcrumbs
500g (1lb 2oz) mozzarella or scamorza,
 well-drained and cut into 1cm (½in)
 slices
25g (1oz) butter, plus extra for greasing
salt and freshly ground black pepper

Try to find anelli pasta for this – they look like little hoops (just like canned spaghetti hoops). They are small but, cooked al dente, should hold their shape when you come to unbuckle the cake tin and invert this masterpiece on to a plate. Everyone will watch you, goggle-eyed: Will it? Won't it? It should, if you've buttered and breadcrumbed with due caution and care. The reveal is always a little nerve-wracking, but only enough to keep you on your toes.

1. Preheat the oven to 190°C/180°C fan/375°F/Gas 5. Grease a 28cm (11¼in) diameter and 10cm (4in) deep springform cake tin with butter and line a baking sheet with baking paper.

2. Toss the aubergine, tomatoes and 3 tablespoons of the olive oil together in a bowl. Season well with salt and pepper and arrange the aubergine and tomatoes in an even layer on the lined baking sheet. Bake for about 15–20 minutes, until soft and beginning to colour in places.

3. Meanwhile, prepare the sauce. Heat 2 tablespoons of the remaining olive oil in a pan over a moderate heat. Add the onion and fry for about 10 minutes, until softened but not coloured, then add the garlic and cook for 2 minutes, until fragrant. Add the oregano and the passata and season well with salt and pepper. Cook for about 10 minutes, until rich and thick.

4. Meanwhile, boil the pasta in well-salted water for 4–5 minutes, keeping it firmly al dente. Drain, and add the pasta to the tomato sauce. Add the remaining 1 tablespoon of olive oil, stirring well to coat, then add half the pecorino or Parmesan and all the aubergine and tomato.

5. Reserve 1 tablespoon of the breadcrumbs and sprinkle the remainder into the greased cake tin, tapping the tin around and from side to side to ensure you coat the entire inside surface with an even layer of crumbs.

6. Half fill the tin with the pasta mixture, pressing down to compact it. Arrange the mozzarella or scamorza on top in a layer, then sprinkle with all but 1 tablespoon of the remaining pecorino or Parmesan. Add a final layer of pasta mixture, pressing down firmly to compact.

7. Sprinkle the pasta with the reserved tablespoon of breadcrumbs and the remaining Parmesan or pecorino and dot it all with the butter.

8. Bake the timballo for about 30 minutes, until the top is golden and almost firm to the touch. Remove from the oven and let the timballo rest in the tin for 5–10 minutes before inverting it out on to a large serving plate to slice. Sprinkle with more pecorino or Parmesan, if you like.

Whole Tomato Kofte

50g (1¾oz) coarse bulgur wheat
16 tomatoes, halved horizontally
500g (1lb 2oz) minced (ground) lamb
  or beef
½ onion, very finely diced
30g (1oz) butter
4 garlic cloves: 3 thinly sliced, 1 halved
200g (7oz) passata or 200g (7oz)
  canned chopped tomatoes
salt and freshly ground black pepper

For the chopped salad
½–1 cucumber, finely diced
1 pomegranate, seeds removed
½–1 large red or green (bell) pepper,
  deseeded and finely diced

a small bunch of flat-leaf parsley or mint,
  leaves picked and roughly chopped
juice of ½ lemon

To serve
flat breads (such as pide or lavash,
  or pita)
150g (5½oz) full-fat natural (plain)
  yogurt, seasoned with a good pinch
  of salt
pickles
½ lemon, cut into wedges
chilli flakes (preferably Aleppo or Urfa),
  for sprinkling
ground sumac, for sprinkling

I made these kofte during a live cook-a-long session with Ulrika Johnson, home-cook champion (among many other wonderful things) and my muse at the other end of the camera. The session was a great deal of fun, both of us with a glass of wine in hand, the rain lashing here in Bristol and one or other of my children filming me at a barbecue while holding an umbrella (to no avail – I got soaked). Ulrika looked far more cool, effortlessly stylish, with her dog and youngest daughter as company. I'm aware that sometimes I can cook at such speed (it's the chef in me) that people will struggle to keep up. Ulrika kept pace and the night was a riot, albeit a virtual one, such was the 'thing' in the summer of 2020. Original recipe published by The Tomato Stall (@iowtomatoes) and reprinted here with their kind permission.

1. Tip the bulgur into a pan of salted water and place it over a high heat. Bring to a boil, then reduce the heat and simmer for about 15 minutes, until tender. Remove from the heat, drain and leave to cool in the colander.

2. Scoop out the flesh and seeds of the halved tomatoes, reserving them both, along with any juices, in a bowl. Season the cavities with salt and turn them cavity downward on a plate, to catch any juice.

3. Tip the lamb or beef, the cooled bulgur, the diced onion, a teaspoon of salt and ½ teaspoon of pepper into the bowl of a stand mixer fitted with the beater and mix on high speed for about 2 minutes, until sticky and cohesive. (Alternatively, you can do this by hand.) Put to one side.

continued overleaf

4. Melt the butter in a saucepan over a moderate-low heat. Add the garlic and fry for about 2 minutes, until fragrant. Add the passata or canned tomatoes and any juice from the scooped-out tomatoes. Season with salt and pepper and simmer for at least 15–20 minutes, until thick and rich-tasting. Remove from the heat and put to one side to keep warm.

5. Preheat the grill (broiler) to high and preheat the oven to 200°C/180°C fan/400°F/Gas 6.

6. Pour the tomato sauce into a round, 25cm (10in) baking dish (or something comparable in size).

7. Divide and shape the meat mixture into 16 equal, ping-pong-sized balls. Nestle 1 ball into a scooped-out tomato half and top with another scooped-out half, enveloping the ball. Repeat with the rest of the meatballs and tomato halves. Place each stuffed tomato snugly side by side in the baking dish.

8. Grill (broil) the stuffed tomatoes under the hot grill for 3–5 minutes, until beginning to blister and blacken, then transfer them to the oven and bake for about 8–10 minutes to cook through – a little pink is fine for both lamb and beef, so do cook to your liking. Remove from the oven and leave to rest for 5 minutes or so.

9. While the stuffed tomatoes are resting, combine the chopped salad ingredients, seasoning to taste.

10. To serve, briefly heat the flat breads under a hot grill, then top with the stuffed tomatoes and chopped salad, along with the seasoned yogurt, pickles and lemon wedges, with chilli flakes and sumac to sprinkle.

Tomato, Crème Fraîche and Dijon Cheddar Cobbler

2 tablespoons olive oil
800g (1lb 12oz) tomatoes, cut into
  2cm (¾in) slices
3 thyme sprigs, leaves picked
1 teaspoon Dijon mustard
150g (5½oz) crème fraîche
freshly ground black pepper

For the topping
180g self-raising flour
½ teaspoon salt, plus more to season
130g (4½oz) butter, cubed and chilled
100g (3½oz) cheddar, grated
  (shredded)
3 eggs, beaten
4 tablespoons whole milk

*What could be more tempting than a bubbling mass of tomatoes and crème fraîche
cooked under a blanket of cobbler topping, puffing all crisp and golden. For the best
results, try to spoon the topping on to the tomatoes with a few gaps and pockets of
tomatoes uncovered. Serve with extra Dijon mustard on the side. And, once again,
never piping hot – these dishes are generally best served warm.*

1. Preheat the oven to 180°C/160°C fan/350°F/Gas 4.

2. Heat the olive oil in a frying pan over a moderate–high heat. Add the tomatoes
and half the thyme leaves and season with some salt and pepper. Cook for about
2 minutes at a vigorous simmer, until the tomatoes have sightly collapsed and the
juices have thickened, just a little. Remove from the heat.

3. Make the topping. In a mixing bowl, mix together the flour and salt, then rub in the
butter with your fingertips until the butter is broken up and the mixture resembles
fine breadcrumbs. Stir through the cheese and remaining thyme leaves.

4. In a separate bowl, mix together the eggs and milk. Make a well in the flour
mixture, then tip in the egg and milk mixture and swiftly combine to form a batter.
Don't overwork it. Set aside while you finish the filling.

5. In a small bowl, mix together the mustard and crème fraîche and season well with
salt and pepper. Spread this over the base of a 24cm (9½in) baking dish. Add the
tomatoes with all their juices.

6. With a large serving spoon, drop large spoonfuls of the topping batter all over
the surface of the tomatoes, leaving spaces between the dollops if you can. Bake the
cobbler for about 35 minutes, until the tomatoes are bubbling and the topping is
crisp and golden.

Tomatoes with Chicken and Orzo

SERVES 4

4 large chicken thighs, with or without
  skin (up to you)
3 tablespoons olive oil
2 red (bell) peppers, deseeded and
  thinly sliced
1 onion, thinly sliced
3–4 garlic cloves, thinly sliced
1 tablespoon tomato purée
  (concentrated paste)
½–1 teaspoon chilli flakes, to taste
½–1 teaspoon dried oregano, to taste

½ teaspoon sweet paprika
½ teaspoon salt, plus more to season
500g (1lb 2oz) passata
300g (10½oz) orzo pasta
250ml (9fl oz) hot chicken stock or
  boiling water
½ small bunch of flat-leaf parsley,
  leaves picked and finely chopped
freshly ground black pepper
½ lemon, cut into wedges, to serve

I love orzo; it is without a doubt one of my favourite pasta shapes, notably because of the delightful way in which it cooks – at once slippery and soft, but still with structure and substance that belies its diminutive size. Shaped like a rice grain, it's no surprise that orzo enjoys recipes suited to rice cookery. In passata and chicken stock, the pasta swells with the liquid, cooking to perfection, and, if you're lucky, you might even get a gorgeous golden crust on the base of the dish – like a shield. Serve with lemon wedges.

1. Season the chicken thighs with salt and pepper all over.

2. Heat the oil in a casserole or heavy-based pan with a lid over a moderate heat. Add the chicken and seal for about 4–5 minutes on each side, until nicely coloured. Remove the meat to a plate, keeping any fat and chicken juices back in the pan.

3. Add the peppers and onion to the pan, lower the heat to moderate–low and cook for about 10 minutes, until softened. Add the garlic and cook for a further 2 minutes, until the garlic smells fragrant.

4. Add the tomato purée, chilli flakes, oregano, paprika and the ½ teaspoon of salt. Cook for 1 minute more, then return the chicken thighs to the pan and mix well so that the chicken is coated in the onion mixture. Add the passata and cook for 5 minutes, until rich and thick.

5. Add the orzo to the pan along with the stock or boiling water, turn up the heat to high and bring the liquid to a vigorous simmer. Cover with a lid, reduce the heat to low again and cook for about 25–30 minutes, until the orzo and chicken are both cooked through. Once or twice, give the mixture a little nudge with a wooden spoon, making sure you go all the way to the bottom of the pan, as the orzo can stick.

6. Remove the pan from the heat and allow everything to rest for 5 minutes. Check the seasoning, adding plenty of pepper, and a little more salt if necessary, then stir through the parsley before serving. Serve with lemon wedges for squeezing over.

BAKED & ROASTED

Tomato and Filo Pie with Honey and Walnuts

butter, for greasing
200g (7oz) feta, crumbled
225g (8oz) halloumi, coarsely grated (shredded)
50g (1¾oz) Parmesan or cheddar, coarsely grated (shredded)
400g (14oz) tomatoes, coarsely grated (shredded), including the skin
2 eggs
½ teaspoon dried oregano

1 x 300–350g (10½–12oz) packet of filo (phyllo) pastry, cut into 7.5cm (3in) ribbons
175ml (5½fl oz) double (heavy) cream
175ml (5½fl oz) whole milk
30g (1oz) walnuts pieces, roughly crushed
2 tablespoons olive oil
about 2 tablespoons honey, for drizzling
salt and freshly ground black pepper

This recipe is inspired by a recipe in Georgina Hayden's book Taverna, *in which she uses courgettes (zucchini), and it reminds me of the Greek and Cypriot cheese pies made with kataifi pastry. However, kataifi is hard to come by in non-specialist shops, so I've substituted filo, which I have sliced into ribbons to mirror kataifi pastry, an excellent kitchen task and a pleasing job to do, especially if you buy the filo that comes in a roll. Some of the pastry soaks in the cream and cheese and some bakes golden and crisp, to drizzle with runny honey and walnuts. It is important that you bake the pie in a tin that sits on the bottom of the oven to cook, which ensures that the pastry beneath browns beautifully. This is a great bake for a picnic or long, lazy lunch outside, in the sunshine.*

1. Grease 30 x 20cm (12 x 8in) metal baking tin with butter.

2. In a large mixing bowl, combine the feta, halloumi, Parmesan or cheddar and tomatoes. Add one of the eggs and the oregano and season with salt and plenty of pepper, remembering that the cheese can be salty.

3. Arrange half the tangle of sliced filo into the dish, pushing it up the sides as well, as best you can. Add the grated cheese and tomato mixture, then arrange the remaining filo over the top to cover.

4. In a separate mixing bowl, whisk together the cream, milk and remaining egg and pour this mixture over the pie. Leave to one side for 30 minutes before baking. Meanwhile, preheat the oven to 180°C/160°C fan/350°F/Gas 4.

5. With the oven hot and the pie well soaked, scatter over the walnuts and drizzle with the olive oil. Place the dish directly on the bottom of the oven and bake for 35 minutes, until crisp and golden. If you think the top needs a little more colour, pop the dish on the top shelf of the oven and continue baking for about 10 minutes, then remove it from the oven and drizzle with the honey, leaving the pie to sit for at least 10 minutes before serving.

Tomato and Mozzarella Lasagne

3 tablespoons olive oil
1 large onion, finely diced
4 garlic cloves, finely chopped
3 x 400g (14oz) cans of cherry tomatoes
1 teaspoon dried oregano, or fresh basil,
   oregano, marjoram or rosemary leaves,
   finely chopped
salt and freshly ground black pepper

For the béchamel
60g (2oz) butter, plus extra for greasing

60g (2oz) plain (all-purpose) flour
800ml (28fl oz) whole milk
freshly grated nutmeg, to taste

To assemble
3 x 125g (4½oz) balls of mozzarella, well
   drained and thinly sliced
about 9-12 sheets of egg lasagne
100g (3½oz) Parmesan, grated
   (shredded)

What a way to finish an entire book on tomatoes – a lasagne to rival all others. Or, at the very least, make all who sit waiting at the table draw breath and marvel in the moment. Lasagne is – hands down – my daughter Grace's favourite dinner. This version came to be for Grace, her vegetarianism gaining in momentum, her love for lasagne never dwindling. I'm doing away with the meat ragù here and instead opting for good, canned tomatoes (in this case, canned cherry tomatoes are best, I find, for a bit of structure), mozzarella, béchamel and Parmesan. This version is a thing of beauty. And, remember, like the Earth's tectonic plates shifting into position, lasagne needs a good rest for the layers to hold up and the cheese to really relax and stretch before you serve it.

1. Heat the oil in a large saucepan over a moderate heat. Fry the onion for 10 minutes, until softened but not coloured. Add the garlic and cook for 2 minutes, until fragrant.

2. Add the canned tomatoes and the herbs, and season well with salt and pepper. Cook for 15 minutes for the flavours to meld and the contents of the pan to thicken. Check the seasoning, adding more salt and pepper, if needed. Remove from the heat.

3. Make the béchamel. Melt the butter in a large saucepan over a moderate heat. Add the flour and, stirring briskly, cook for 2 minutes, until amalgamated and the mixture is beginning to fur up on the bottom of the pan. Add the milk in a steady stream, whisking all the time, and bringing the contents of the pan to a boil. Then, reduce the heat and season with salt and pepper and plenty of nutmeg. Cook at a gentle simmer for 5-8 minutes, until the sauce is smooth and thick. Remove from the heat.

4. Preheat the oven to 180°C/160°C fan/350°F/Gas 4.

5. Grease a 30 x 20cm (12 x 8in) baking dish with a little butter and add one third of the tomato sauce to the bottom of the dish. Arrange one third of the mozzarella over the tomatoes, top with 3-4 sheets of lasagne, then cover with one third of the béchamel sauce. Scatter over one third of the Parmesan. Repeat the process twice more, finishing with the final one third of Parmesan.

6. Bake for 35-40 minutes, until bubbling at the sides and golden brown on top. Remove from the oven and leave to rest for about 10 minutes before serving.

I wrote this book, and these people worked tirelessly to make it.

Sam Folan
Photographer and friend.
Matthew Williamson
Recipe developer and partner in everything.
Grace Williamson
Recipe taster #1: a winning and enthusiastic attitude to food and cooking.
Ivy Williamson
Recipe taster #2: daring and plucky, and always the first to ask, 'what's for dinner?'
Dorothy Williamson
Recipe taster #3: never underestimated, and fearless in the face of so many tomatoes.
Faye Wears
Prop stylist wonder woman.
Judy Barratt
Red pen-wielding shapeshifter.
Harriet Webster
Editor at large.
Claire Rochford
Design is everything.

Thanks to:

Isle of Wight Tomatoes
An unstinting supply of beautiful seasonal tomatoes.
Mutti
For when the season came to an end, very best, and storecupboard staple.
Fish for Thought
Sustainably caught fish, direct to your door.
Pipers Farm
Online butcher, nothing too much trouble.

FURTHER READING

Jane Grigson's Vegetable Book
Jane Grigson

On Food and Cooking: an encyclopedia of kitchen science, history and culture
Harold McGee

The Flavour Thesaurus: pairings, recipes and ideas for the creative cook
Niki Segnit

Vegetables
Roger Phillips and Martyn Rix

Tomato: a global history
Clarissa Hyman

The Oxford Companion to Italian Food
Gillian Riley

British Tomato Growers' Association
www.britishtomatoes.co.uk

Managing Director Sarah Lavelle
Commissioning Editor Harriet Webster
Copy-editor Judy Barratt
Head of Design Claire Rochford
Food Stylists Claire Thomson and
  Matt Williamson
Photographer Sam Folan
Prop Stylist Faye Wears
Head of Production Stephen Lang
Production Controller Katie Jarvis

Published in 2022 by Quadrille,
an imprint of Hardie Grant Publishing

Quadrille
52–54 Southwark Street
London SE1 1UN
quadrille.com

Cataloguing in Publication Data: a catalogue record for this book is
available from The British Library.

The publisher has made every effort to trace the copyright holders.
We apologize in advance for any unintentional omissions and would
be pleased to insert the appropriate acknowledgement in any
subsequent edition.

Text © Claire Thomson 2022
Photography © Sam Folan 2022
Design © Quadrille 2022

Quote on page 7 taken from *Jane Grigson's
Vegetable Book* by Jane Grigson (current
edition published by Penguin, 1998)

ISBN 978 1 78713 785 1

Reprinted in 2022, 2023
10 9 8 7 6 5 4 3

Printed in China